South Africa: The Sanctions Mission

South Africa:
The Sanctions Mission

Report of the Eminent Church Persons Group

Prepared by Dr James Mutambirwa

World Council of Churches
Geneva

Zed Books Ltd
London and New Jersey

South Africa: The Sanctions Mission was first published in 1989 by:
Zed Books Ltd, 57 Caledonian Road, London N1 9BU and
171 First Avenue, Atlantic Highlands, New Jersey 07716
with
The World Council of Churches,
150 Route de Ferney, PO Box No. 66, 1211 Geneva 20

Copyright © WCC, 1989

Cover design by Andrew Corbett
Typeset by EMS Photosetters, Rochford, Essex
Printed and bound in United Kingdom by
Cox and Wyman Ltd, Reading

British Library Cataloguing in Publication Data

South Africa : the sanction mission : a report to
the World Council of Churches
1. International relations. Role of World
Council of Churches
I. World Council of Churches *Eminent Church
Persons' Group*
261.8'7

ISBN 0-86232-910-8
ISBN 0-86232-911-6 pbk

Contents

Photographs appear on pp. xiii–xvi

Members of the Eminent Church Persons Group: Biographical Details

Rev. Dr Canaan Banana of Zimbabwe

Rev. Dr Banana obtained a Diploma in Theology at the Epworth Theological College and in 1962 was ordained into the ministry of the Methodist Church (UK). He has been a pastor and an acting principal of a boarding school. Due to his involvement in the Zimbabwean liberation struggle, he was forced to leave Rhodesia in 1973 and was briefly a refugee in Botswana. Later that year he obtained a scholarship to study at Wesley Theological Seminary in Washington D.C. where he received his M.Th. degree. Rev. Banana is also the recipient of three honorary doctorate degrees.

When he returned to Rhodesia in May 1975, he was arrested and sentenced to three months' imprisonment. In January 1976 he was released but was restricted to an area within a 15-mile radius of Bulawayo. He was detained again in January 1977 and held in the Wha Wha detention camp until November 1979. On 17 April 1980 he was sworn in as the first President of Zimbabwe.

Rev. Banana retired from the Presidency in December 1987. Since then he has been teaching at the United Theological College in Harare and at the University of Zimbabwe where he is Professor of Religious Studies and Philosophy. He has written several books, among them *Towards a Socialist Ethos* and *Theology of Promise*.

Ms Elaine Hesse Greif, General Secretary of the World Young Women's Christian Association (YWCA)

Ms Hesse Greif was born and raised in California USA; she completed a degree in history at Mills College and, as a post-graduate student, studied South Asian land reform at the University of California, Berkeley.

She moved to Aotearoa/New Zealand in 1968. In both countries she has been involved professionally in social welfare and education and as a volunteer with the YWCA. Her last appointment in Aotearoa/New Zealand was as Principal of St Hilda's Collegiate School in Dunedin.

In January 1987 she took up office as the General Secretary of the World YWCA. She is a member of the Anglican Church.

Dr Lysaneas Maciel of Brazil

Dr Maciel is a lawyer and legal counsel to the Brazilian Ministry of Labour. Under the military governments from 1964 to the 1980s, he acted for both urban and rural working-class detainees. He also founded and was director of a Centre for Social Care of Children, looking after those between two and six years old from the slums of Rio.

He is an elected deputy in the Brazilian National Congress, now serving his third term. He is also President of the Commission for Energy in the Chamber of Deputies and rapporteur of the Commission for Collective Rights and Sovereignty of the National Assembly, which body in 1988 promulgated a new Constitution.

He was an officer of the Commission on Inter-Church Aid, Refugee and World Service (CICARWS) with the World Council of Churches during the late 1970s. He has written several books, including *Alternative to Despair*, *Church Presence and Tensions*, *The Nature of the Opposition in a Dictatorial Regime*.

Metropolitan Paulos Mar Gregorios of India

Paulos Mar Gregorios is the Metropolitan of Delhi for the

Orthodox Church of the East. Since 1967 he has also been Principal of the Orthodox Seminary in Kottayam, Kerala, India. Prior to this, he was an Associate General Secretary of the WCC and Director of the Division of Ecumenical Action. He is currently one of the Presidents of the WCC.

He served on the personal staff of Emperor Haile Selassie (1956–59) as chief adviser to his Welfare Foundation and executive secretary to the committee for the distribution of relief aid. During this period, he was honorary lecturer in religion at the University College of Addis Ababa. He initially went to Ethiopia to teach English and mathematics in government schools.

In his youth the Metropolitan worked for five years on a daily newspaper in Kerala, his home state. He was the General Secretary of the Orthodox Christian Student Movement in India (1954–57), and Honorary Associate Secretary of the Student Christian Movement of India.

He graduated with a BA from Goshen College, Indiana, USA (1952), and received his M.Div. from Princeton Theological Seminary (1954). In 1960 he received the STM degree from Yale University Divinity School. He has also studied at Oxford University and the University of Minster. He took his doctorate in theology at Serampore University in India. He has honorary doctorates from the Universities of Leningrad, Budapest and Prague. He is also General President of the Indian Philosophical Congress. He was moderator of the WCC sub-unit on Church and Society (1975–83), and chaired the World Conference on Faith, Science and the Future in Boston, USA, in 1979. He is the author of a dozen books including *The Human Presence*, *Cosmic Man*, and *Science for some Societies*.

Rev. Dr Carl Mau of the United States

Dr Mau is a former General Secretary of the Lutheran World Federation (LWF). He obtained his BA from Washington State University in 1944 and his Master of Divinity degree from the Lutheran Seminary in Philadelphia. Since then he has pursued additional graduate studies in USA and Europe, as well as being awarded honorary degrees in both West Germany and the United States.

He was ordained a pastor of the Lutheran Church in 1946 and took up his first post with the Lutheran Memorial Church in Portland, Oregon, USA. Between 1950 and 1956 he was the representative of the LWF's Department of World Service and Inter-Church Aid in Hanover, West Germany. He has also held posts as Associate General Secretary of the Lutheran World Federation in Geneva, Switzerland, as General Secretary of the USA National Committee of LWF in New York and between 1974 and 1985 he held the post of LWF General Secretary in Geneva.

He is now Chief Executive and Ecumenical Officer of LWF and a member of several boards, such as the Strasbourg Institute. He has attended six of the seven LWF Assemblies and been responsible for organizing the last four. He has represented LWF in numerous world gatherings and been a member of delegations to various parts of the world.

His articles and reports have been published in English and German periodicals and journals. He lectures in Lutheran churches, faculties and synods throughout the world and has participated in radio and television programmes. His honours include the Wichern Medal of the Evangelical Church of Germany; the Legion of Merit Cross of the German Federal Republic and a special citation from the Federal Bureau of Prisons, USA.

Rev. Dr Beyers Naudé of South Africa

Dr Naudé was born into an Afrikaans-speaking family in South Africa. He began theological studies in 1932 at Stellenbosch University, a cradle of Afrikaner nationalism and the *alma mater* to six of South Africa's eight prime ministers. After completing his studies, he became an ordained minister in the Dutch Reformed Church (NGK) in 1940, serving several congregations in the Cape and the Transvaal. That same year he was formally inducted into a local *Broederbond* cell and swore on the Bible an oath of fidelity to the aspirations of the Afrikaner people.

In 1949 he was appointed student pastor at the University of Pretoria, from where he began to question the racial dogmas of the Afrikaner people. In 1954, after becoming pastor of a congregation in Potchefstroom, he began a study of scripture and theology in regard to Church, society and race.

In May 1962, he launched a monthly magazine, *Pro Veritate*, whose editorial board included a number of respected Afrikaner theologians. From the outset its articles on race, ecumenism, and religious–political matters differed radically from the official NGK viewpoint. Despite an official campaign against him, large sections of the NGK supported Naudé. Increasingly dissatisfied with the Church's failure to speak out on national issues, particularly on the racial question, Naudé took the initiative of establishing a formal ecumenical structure to demonstrate the unity of Christ's Church across the boundaries of race and denomination. On 13 August 1963, the Christian Institute was launched and Naudé was asked to be its full-time director. A month later, faced by a statement from the NGK Church hierarchy that he no longer had their support, he left the NGK ministry.

In 1974, the government revoked his passport. The following year, the Le Grange Commission of Enquiry determined that the Christian Institute would not be permitted to receive funds from outside the country. In 1976, Beyers Naudé was jailed for his refusal to give secret testimony to a state commission; he had been willing to testify but only in a public setting. Issues of *Pro Veritate* were frequently banned and, in 1977, the Christian Institute was banned. Dr Naudé was himself put under a banning order that restricted him to Johannesburg, barred his involvement in meetings, and required that neither his words nor writings could be published. This order remained in force for more than seven years.

In January 1985, he was appointed General Secretary of the South African Council of Churches, succeeding Archbishop Desmond Tutu. Though now retired, he remains a tireless spokesperson against apartheid, travelling, writing and speaking in public.

Dr Lucille Mair of Jamaica

Dr Mair is a former Deputy Secretary-General of the United Nations. She was Dean of Students at the University of the West Indies for 17 years before being appointed Secretary-General of the UN Mid-Decade Conference on Women, held in Mexico. Later she was appointed Secretary-General of the UN Conference on the Question of Palestine. She is currently Co-ordinator of the Women's Development Unit of the University of the West Indies. Dr Mair was elected a Senator in February 1989 and is now Minister of State for Foreign Affairs in Jamaica.

Resource Persons for the Members of the Eminent Church Persons Group

Rev. Frank Chikane of South Africa

Rev. Frank Chikane was born in Johannesburg in 1951 and was ordained a pastor of the Apostolic Faith Mission in charge of a congregation in Krugersdorp. He remained there for about $5\frac{1}{2}$ years, during a volatile period of South Africa's political history. Responding to the situation around him, he was first detained in January 1977 and has since been detained and tortured on a number of subsequent occasions. From November 1981 to July 1982, he was detained and kept in solitary confinement. As a result of his work for social justice, he has been increasingly at loggerheads with his Church.

He was active in Soweto community life as Deputy President of the Soweto Civic Association between 1984 and 1987 and was a Vice-President of the Transvaal Region of the United Democratic Front (UDF) between 1983 and 1985. Since 1981 he has worked with the Institute of Contextual Theology (ICT) becoming its General Secretary in 1983. ICT is an institute which attempts to develop a theology relevant to the context of South Africa. This has involved him in writing theology with young blacks and meeting with a range of community organizations and independent churches in Soweto. In 1985 he played a major role in drafting the *Kairos Document*, an assessment of the apartheid situation in South Africa.

He was eventually charged with treason for his involvement in the United Democratic Front. In 1987 he received a peace prize from Diakonia, an aid organization of the Swedish Free Churches, for his work on peace and justice.

Since July 1987 he has been the General Secretary of the South African Council of Churches. Rev. Chikane has written an autobiography, *No Life of my Own*.

Dr James Mutambirwa of Zimbabwe

Dr Mutambirwa is Programme Secretary of the Commission on the Programme to Combat Racism (PCR) of the World Council of Churches.

He has a doctorate from Columbia University in the United States. He has taught in Zimbabwe and the United States where he was on the staff of Rutgers University during the 1970s.

He is the author of many articles and research documents on Southern Africa, and Zimbabwe in particular, and his book *The Rise of Settler Power in Southern Rhodesia* was published in 1980. He has organized a number of major gatherings of church leaders from all over the world.

Rev. Bob Scott of Aotearoa/New Zealand

Rev. Bob Scott, an Anglican priest from Aotearoa/New Zealand, was appointed to the PCR staff in October 1988. During the 1970s, he was director of an inner-city ecumenical team ministry in Aotearoa/New Zealand. That was followed by a period as Executive Secretary of the International Coalition for Development Action (ICDA) based in London. He worked with an information project, focused on the North–South dialogue, at the United Nations in New York from 1980 to 1982. He then returned to Aotearoa/New Zealand to join the staff of the National Council of Churches and be responsible for that country's first full-time programme on racism.

WCC Photo: Peter Williams

Left to right: Dr Lysaneas Maciel, Rev. N. Pityana, Ms Elaine Hesse Greif, Rev. Canaan Banana, Dr James Mutambirwa, Rev. Frank Chikane

Mr Damu Smith (standing), Executive Director of the Washington Office on Africa (WOA) briefing the ECPG on the US Congress and Southern Africa

New York: Eminent Church Persons Group meeting with Xavier Pérez de Cuellar, Secretary-General of the United Nations (fourth from right)

FREIHEIT FÜR SÜDAFRIKA UND NAMIBIA

Eminent Church Persons Group singing 'We Shall Overcome' at the end of the meeting with 150 anti-apartheid action groups at the Academy Mulheim in Germany

Foreword

The Republic of South Africa stands guilty in the world arena because of its ideology of apartheid, one that has given rise to a pseudo-religious political and economic system which works violence, poverty, degradation and marginalization because of the colour of people's skin. The Christian world, by and large, has condemned apartheid as a heresy.

The Christian gospel does not permit Christians to be satisfied with only finding fault with and condemning the wayward but requires them to go on to seek their salvation in diverse ways and to restore them to the community of humankind, the *raison d'être* of the ecumenical movement. Hence, since 1948, but particularly since the Uppsala Assembly of 1968, the World Council of Churches (WCC) has had racism and the Republic of South Africa on its agenda. It is also in the context of that concern for the Republic of South Africa that the Eminent Church Persons Group (ECPG) was sent to the major cities of the Western world to sue for peace with justice in that embattled and tragic region.

The mandate for this particular project came from a meeting in May 1987 in Lusaka, Zambia on 'A Struggle for Justice is a Struggle for Peace: The Churches' Search for Justice and Peace in Southern Africa'. Here there were some 250 delegates, including about 70 from South Africa and Namibia. But more than that, the involvement flows from the WCC's *raison d'être* as an agent of God's mission. The central message of that mission is the kingdom of God and its characteristics include

1

love, truth, righteousness and justice, freedom, reconciliation and peace. On each of these criteria, the situation in the Republic of South Africa poses problems and challenges.

For years signs of meaningful change in South Africa have been difficult to discern. So, despite what the government of South Africa claims, compulsory sanctions as a tool to bring pressure for change has been advocated in world forums by church persons and politicians from within and without South Africa. Inside the country we need specifically to cite the Congress of South African Trade Unions (COSATU) and the National Council of Trade Unions (NACTU), both of which have pressed for the imposition of sanctions.

In January and February 1989, the Eminent Church Persons Group (ECPG) visited the major countries of the world involved in trade with South Africa to urge sanctions, not as an irresponsible punitive measure but as painful medicine to be administered in the interests of the health of the Republic and the community of humanity. Let me repeat that the advocacy for sanctions, so far as the WCC is concerned, is not seen as a punitive measure; rather, it is seen as an alternative to the violence of apartheid; it is for the sake of the victims of apartheid as well as out of a desire that we all get to the messianic banquet together. But that is impossible without a change of ideology and amendment of life, making for a real and general community of humanity in which the kingdom's values are lived, where the integrity and dignity of each and every human being is respected so that the good news of the image and likeness of God, that is in each and every human being, may become a real gospel of hope.

It is my great pleasure to thank the Eminent Church Persons Group (ECPG) for undertaking this onerous and delicate task for the world church. They are busy and responsible persons and they made sacrifices to be on this assignment. Words are inadequate to express our gratitude, but we will still use a familiar 'thank you', expressed with deep feeling.

At the same time let me express the hope that the governments visited have heard the message and will see the moral necessity to pursue the measures that will not only avoid a violent bloodbath in South Africa, but also help to end the pain of the victims of apartheid.

2

Let me dare to express the hope that posterity will come to say that this ECPG's work advanced the day of peace with justice and reconciliation.

Emilio Castro

General Secretary
World Council of Churches
Geneva

June 1989

Introduction

The Memorandum of the Eminent Church Persons Group of the World Council of Churches

The Eminent Church Persons Group was mandated by the Executive Committee of the World Council of Churches, meeting in Atlanta in 1987, to visit specific governments to urge the implementation of appropriate UN resolutions regarding South Africa and the imposition of sanctions by them.

For the last 20 years Southern Africa has been one of the major priorities of the WCC as it sought to educate and mobilize the international church community against apartheid and white minority rule in the region. From the beginning of its actions to end white minority rule, WCC anti-racist activities have been rooted in economic measures. At the Fourth General Assembly (Uppsala, 1968), in its first important anti-apartheid action, the WCC delegates decided that all investments in 'institutions that perpetuate racism' should be terminated. In 1972, four years later, the WCC Central Committee put these words into action and instructed its Finance Committee to sell its investments in corporations directly involved in investing and trading with those countries in Southern Africa practising racial discrimination and to deposit no funds in banks which maintain direct banking operations in those countries.

The resolution read:

> Considering the effect of foreign investments in Southern Africa to strengthen the white minority regime in their oppression of the majority of the people of the region, and implementing the policy as commended by the WCC Assembly in Uppsala (1968) that investments in 'institutions that perpetuate racism' should be

5

terminated; urges all member churches, Christian agencies and individual Christians outside South Africa to use all their influence, including stockbroker action and disinvestment, to press corporations to withdraw investments from and cease trading with these countries.

Since then the WCC has been concerned to support actions by the UN, Commonwealth and other international agencies seeking to bring apartheid to an end.

In Lusaka, in May 1987, 250 church leaders from around the world (including strong representation from South Africa) called for the setting up of an Eminent Church Persons Group to visit specific nations with a high level of economic ties with the government to South Africa. That meeting emphasized the urgency of such a Group because of:

i) the deteriorating political situation in South Africa;

ii) the ever-increasing murders, political assassinations, state terrorism and brutality including the imprisonment, torture and murders of children by the State;

iii) the denial of human rights and the perpetuation of apartheid's reign of terror;

iv) the intransigence and unwillingness of the regime in South Africa to abolish apartheid which is a monstrous system characterized by the international community as a crime against humanity and which has caused incalculable losses of life and property both inside and outside South Africa itself, and

v) the recognition that apartheid is the only cause of the present conflicts in the whole of Southern Africa, which conflicts have resulted in the sad and tragic murders and mutilations of innocent civilians in the Frontline States.

Once established, the ECPG met with government leaders to give expression to the above view that apartheid must end. It spoke in the knowledge that it reflected the resolutions and decisions of 307 member churches from over 150 countries. It argued that the apartheid system must be abolished *in toto*. Apartheid has caused misery, suffering, pain and death for the peoples of South Africa and the neighbouring states. All peace-loving people in the world agree that apartheid is a crime against humanity. The system cannot be reformed, and we cannot wait. For all Christians this is a gospel imperative, as Luke writes in Chapter 4:18: 'He has sent me to proclaim release to the captives, and recovering of sight to the blind, to set at liberty those who are oppressed . . .' It was its view therefore that churches have a moral responsibility to do everything possible to end apartheid now as a response to this Gospel imperative.

The ECPG was aware that many efforts to confront and abolish apartheid have been made in the past. Of special significance was the Commonwealth Eminent Persons Group's mission to South Africa in 1986. After strenuous efforts, that body concluded that the South African government was 'not yet prepared to negotiate fundamental change'.

In setting out on its mission, the ECPG was aware that, despite these and other efforts, nothing had changed substantially in South Africa. On the contrary, the situation had worsened with the tightening of the state of emergency, increased press censorship, and the banning of more anti-apartheid organizations and individuals. The ECPG regarded its mission to government leaders as being most timely, for it believed that the world could not wait whilst the apartheid regime continued to cause such pain and suffering. The Group believed that the primary source of the violence in South Africa was the apartheid system, violence which had now gone beyond the borders of South Africa and was being expressed in the form of aggressive destabilization policies towards the Frontline States. Over 150 world church representatives from 42 countries, including those from Southern Africa, heard graphic details of the effect of those policies at a special WCC meeting in Harare in November 1988.

The ECPG's view was that, unless concerted action was taken, in the words of the Commonwealth Eminent Persons Group, there 'could be the worst bloodbath since the Second World War'. To avert that bloodbath the necessary conditions to bring the South African government to the negotiating table with the legitimate and authentic leadership of the people of South Africa had to be created. This is the responsibility of all individuals, churches and nations.

The ECPG believes that for this to happen it is essential to create a balance of power within the country so that the government will not be able to continue its state terrorism against the oppressed majority, with enormous costs politically, economically and in terms of human life. There must be no option for the South African Government but to enter into genuine negotiations.

To bring about concerted political and economic pressure, the ECPG believes that specific actions must be taken. These must include:

i) Comprehensive mandatory sanctions, including no re-scheduling of loans and a refusal of new loans; a halt to government-guaranteed trade credits; embargoes on oil, coal and strategic minerals; ceasing the exchange with South Africa of intelligence information; and denying landing rights to South African Airways and ending flights to South Africa;

ii) Withdrawing and ending investments in South Africa, and cancelling all licences and franchise agreements;

iii) Isolating South Africa in the diplomatic and cultural fields and in sport;

iv) Recognizing the authentic voice of the people;

v) Demanding the withdrawal of the *Disclosure of Foreign Funds Bill* currently under discussion in the South African Parliament;

vi) Giving economic and military support to the Frontline States.

The Group expects governments visited to undertake the following measures:

i) to work actively for the elimination of apartheid rather than merely stating their abhorrence of it;

ii) to commit themselves to the application of the above measures and communicate this commitment through a *Statement of Intent* to enforce them;

iii) to create national and international monitoring mechanisms for the sanctions already imposed and to stop all forms of sanctions-busting. When corporations or individuals withdraw their investments or business from South Africa, international attention should be drawn to any country or business taking advantage of the situation.

The ECPG believes that these are some of the immediate measures that will ensure the demise of apartheid by causing the South African government:

i) to terminate the state of emergency and all related restrictions on the media, organizations and leaders of the people;

ii) to release unconditionally Mr Nelson Mandela and all political prisoners and detainees;

iii) to un-ban all political organizations and allow freedom of expression and association;

iv) to enter into negotiations with the legitimate and authentic leaders of the people of South Africa.

The Group is convinced that the application of these measures is the only effective method to bring about peaceful change in South Africa and the establishment of a free and democratic South Africa.

1. The Mandate

The mandate of the Eminent Church Persons Group (ECPG) originated in a WCC Programme to Combat Racism meeting held in Lusaka in May 1987. For the first time, this gathering brought international church leaders into direct dialogue with the leaders of the Southern African liberation movements, the African National Congress (ANC), Pan-Africanist Congress (PAC), and South West Africa People's Organization (SWAPO). Under the theme the 'Struggle for Justice is the Struggle for Peace: the Churches' Search for Justice and Peace in Southern Africa', over 250 delegates and journalists, including 42 delegates from South Africa and 28 from Namibia, attended the meeting. Once again this WCC meeting called 'for the immediate implementation of comprehensive economic sanctions against South Africa.'

The meeting noted that, since the 1985 Harare Declaration, the situation in South Africa had deteriorated further. The participants confessed that they had not done enough to implement the resolutions of previous WCC meetings on South Africa. 'We as churches also recognize and repent of our failure to work as vigorously as possible for the implementation of the Harare Declaration as a basis for bringing the present regime in South Africa and Namibia to an end.' (see *The Churches' Search for Justice and Peace in Southern Africa*, 1987, p. 28). On this occasion the meeting recommended that 'the WCC should send a delegation to major countries which are in trade with South Africa' to call upon their governments and the European

Community to impose comprehensive sanctions on the South African government.

Later, in September 1987, the Executive Committee of the WCC, meeting in Atlanta, USA, endorsed the resolution. This was the first time that the WCC had decided on an instrument like an Eminent Church Persons Group to persuade the major trading partners of South Africa to adopt mandatory sanctions against that country.

Meanwhile, the situation in South Africa continued to deteriorate. In February 1988, 17 non-violent anti-apartheid organizations were banned. By the end of the year the number had increased to 32. In August 1988 Khotso House, the headquarters of the South African Council of Churches (SACC), was destroyed by the largest bomb ever exploded in South Africa. Kanya House, headquarters of the Southern African Catholic Bishops Conference (SACBC), was also destroyed by arson. In September, a group of church leaders called for an emergency meeting in Geneva with the WCC and church leaders from Europe and North America. The South Africans called upon the WCC, as a matter of extreme urgency, to send the ECPG on its mission.

At a meeting of the Frontline States, organized by the World Council of Churches' Programme to Combat Racism in November 1988, the Most Rev. Walter Khotso Makhulu, Archbishop of Central Africa and one of the seven Presidents of the WCC, suggested in his opening address as moderator of the meeting that the WCC should convene no further meetings on Southern Africa until the ECPG had undertaken its mission.

The importance of the ECPG should not be underestimated. Its mandate emanated from the long history of the WCC's struggle to abolish apartheid, and its task was to articulate the deep concern of the WCC at the grave and explosive crisis that existed in South Africa. Likewise, it was to remind the governments it visited of the Christian imperative to side with the oppressed; this was their Christian responsibility. The mission of the ECPG was the culmination of the efforts that the WCC had undertaken on behalf of the oppressed black majority in South Africa since 1948. It constituted a further universal expression of the WCC's solidarity with the victims of apartheid; it was part of the continuing WCC struggle to eliminate apartheid and an assurance that the WCC would stay the course until that goal was attained.

The ECPG undertook its mission in the 40th anniversary year of the United Nations' Declaration on Human Rights, and the 40th anniversary of the WCC itself. Its mandate was thus the culmination of 40 years of work.

The Lusaka Statement and the ECPG

As stated, the idea for an ECPG Mission was first raised at the PCR/WCC Lusaka meeting of May 1987. Here delegates from South Africa and Namibia told harrowing stories of life under apartheid. South Africa was still under a state of emergency; strict censorship had been imposed and the outside world was being cut off from news of what was happening in the country; over 3,000 people had been killed since September 1984.

In his opening address, the moderator, the Most Rev. Khotso Makhulu, Archbishop of Central Africa, said 'during the last eighteen months the regime in South Africa has descended to new depths of degradation. Some 20,000 opponents of the apartheid regime have been under detention, some of them as young as seven. The emergency powers of the regime have placed South Africa under virtual martial law'. And Dr Beyers Naudé, South African Council of Churches' former General Secretary, said 'the crisis in South Africa is worsening almost daily and the conflict potential is escalating dangerously.' Namibian delegates told of how young people were being tortured by Koevoet, the notoriously brutal police, counter-insurgency unit in Northern Namibia. Exhaust pipes were used to burn people's backs. South African troops were perpetrating rape and murder on black Namibians.

Naudé called upon the international churches to play a more effective role in eradicating apartheid. 'The question of sanctions as a non-violent method of pressuring the South African government to take more effective steps towards fundamental change, should again be seriously considered.' He noted that 'all participants were agreed that apartheid cannot be reformed. It had to be dismantled.'

The Lusaka Statement, which became the basic document of

the Conference, noted, *inter alia*:

> We have heard the moving testimony of the victims of apartheid. The cruel reality of life in the townships of South Africa and the horrors of occupation in Namibia have been brought home to us in the most graphic terms; anguish, suffering, unimaginable pain and heroic resistance are the hallmarks of the struggle for justice in Southern Africa. Against such a background, our duty to ensure that the resolutions that follow are translated into early action is in no doubt . . .
>
> We urgently call upon the churches in countries which, through economic and political cooperation with South Africa and Namibia, support the apartheid regime, to exert increased pressure upon their governments to implement sanctions, and upon banks, corporations and trading institutions to withdraw from doing business with South Africa and Namibia. We especially call upon the international community to apply immediate and comprehensive sanctions to South Africa and Namibia.

The Conference noted that 'in the past, we have failed to move from resolution to practice'. Given the urgency of the situation, it also expressed its determination to see to it that resolute action was taken in order to avoid a catastrophe. The meeting agreed that for the international community the imposition of mandatory economic sanctions was the only peaceful option left in order to ensure a peaceful transition to a democratic multi-racial society in South Africa.

It was against this background that the Lusaka Action Plan was adopted. This called for the establishment of the Eminent Church Persons Group to undertake a mission to seven countries with a high level of economic involvement in South Africa. The mission was specifically to call upon the governments of these countries to impose mandatory economic sanctions against South Africa with the express purpose of forcing the Pretoria regime to the negotiating table with the authentic leaders of the black majority, in the hope that such negotiations would lead to the creation of a new democratic, non-racial South Africa.

On 13 January 1989, members of the ECPG — Rev. Canaan Banana, Ms Elaine Greif and Dr Lysaneas Maciel — were joined by Rev. Frank Chikane, Rev. N. Barney Pityana (Director of the PCR), together with Rev. Bob Scott and Dr

James Mutambirwa as resource persons, at the Hotel du Lac in Coppet near Geneva. For two days this group discussed and developed the strategy of the ECPG mission and drafted a memorandum which explained why the ECPG had been formed and the basis of the message that it would give to the governments they were to visit.

2. The Background: The WCC and Racism

In order to acquire a true perspective of the mission of the Eminent Church Persons Group to seven capitals — Bern, Paris, Brussels, London, Bonn, Tokyo and Washington D.C. — as well as to the headquarters of the United Nations Organization in New York and the European Community in Brussels, between 16 January and 4 February 1989, a brief historical account of the various statements and actions of the World Council of Churches since its inception in 1948 is required.

The World Council of Churches is a committed fellowship of 307 Protestant and Orthodox member churches in over 150 different countries in all continents of the world. Its basis and functions are:

i) to call churches to the goal of visible unity in one faith and in one eucharistic fellowship expressed in worship and in common life in Christ, and to advance towards that unity in order that the world may believe;

ii) to facilitate the common witness of the churches in each place and in all places;

iii) to support the churches in their worldwide missionary and evangelistic task;

iv) to express the common concern of the churches in the service of human need, the breaking down of barriers between people, and the promotion of one human family in justice and peace;

v) to foster the renewal of the churches in unity, worship, mission and service;

vi) to establish and maintain relations with national councils and regional conferences of churches, world confessional bodies and other ecumenical organizations;

vii) to carry on the work of the world movements for Faith and Order and Life and Work and of the International Missionary Council and the World Council in Christian Education.

The WCC is thus committed to seeking the manifest expression of the unity of Christ's Church in the world, and to fostering ecumenical cooperation in the service to all of humanity.

The WCC commissioned the ECPG to visit seven countries with a large volume of trade and economic involvement with South Africa to persuade their leaders to apply comprehensive and mandatory economic and cultural sanctions. The purpose of such sanctions was to put pressure on the white minority regime in South Africa to come to the negotiating table with the authentic leaders of all the people of South Africa and to transfer power to a democratic, non-racial government.

The WCC had not previously used this device of an Eminent Church Persons Group to visit governments and people's organizations in various countries. This extraordinary step was taken because of a global recognition that sanctions were the last means left to the international community to attempt to stop the continuing state violence and violation of human rights in South Africa and avoid a catastrophic eruption of counter-violence and bloodshed. It was also a logical extension of previous WCC statements and actions against apartheid.

Since its formation the World Council of Churches (WCC) has continuously condemned racism. At its first Assembly in Amsterdam in 1948, the WCC stated that:

Churches should call society away from prejudice based upon race or colour and from practices of discrimination and segregation as denials of justice and human dignity. The churches should take a firm and vigorous stand against governments that practise racial discrimination, through local action, in cooperation with churches in other lands, and through international institutions. [This and the following quotations in this chapter are taken from Ans v. der Bent (ed.): *Breaking Down the Walls*, WCC, 1986] (p. 21).

Again in 1954 the Evanston Assembly of the WCC addressed the issue of racism: 'the problems of race, difficult as they are, insoluble as they sometimes appear to be, provide Christians an opportunity for obedience, and for a deeper understanding that bond and free, Jew and Gentile, Greek and Barbarian, people of every land and continent, are all one in Christ' (p. 23). The 1961 Third Assembly of the WCC in New Delhi called upon churches to actively join in the struggle against racial oppression. The Assembly declared that 'where oppression, discrimination and segregation exist, the churches should identify themselves with the oppressed race in its struggle to achieve justice. Christians should be ready to lead in this struggle' (p. 26). In Nairobi in 1975, the Fifth Assembly denounced 'racism as a sin against God and against fellow human beings' (p. 53). In 1966, the World Conference on Church and Society which met in Geneva noted:

It is not enough for churches and groups to condemn the sin of racial arrogance and oppression. The struggle for radical change in structures will inevitably bring suffering and will demand costly and bitter engagement. For Christians to stand aloof from this struggle is to be disobedient to the call of God in history. The meaning of the Cross for our time can be nothing less than this (p. 33).

The Fourth Assembly of the WCC (Uppsala, 1968) warned that 'contemporary racism robs all human rights of their meaning, and is an imminent danger to world peace' (p. 34).

To assist the churches in the struggle against the evil of racism and racial discrimination the WCC in 1969 formed a new sub-unit, the Programme to Combat Racism (PCR). PCR has since become the instrument of the WCC to fight racism of all kinds all over the world, and in particular apartheid in South Africa.

This historical background to the WCC and racism is important. It shows the deep, longstanding and consistent commitment of the WCC to end all forms of racism and racial discrimination. It shows also that the WCC has long recognized that active involvement and engagement in the struggle against racial oppression was not without cost — that it could mean pain and suffering and that it might even be necessary to stand up for the truth and bear the cross if victory over the sin of racism was to be achieved.

Besides making statements and adopting resolutions that denounced apartheid, the WCC has on numerous occasions taken actions to highlight the system's brutality and repression and also to express solidarity with the victims of apartheid. Thus, following the 1960 Sharpeville massacre when 69 people, mostly women and children, were killed by the police — most of them shot in the back — the WCC organized a consultation at Cottesloe, Johannesburg. The consultation was attended by member churches of the WCC in South Africa and by representatives of the WCC secretariat.

The Cottesloe consultation expressed its opposition to all forms of racial discrimination. It noted that 'in a period of rapid social change the church has a special responsibility for fearless witness in society' (p. 24). Significantly, the consultation observed out of its own experience that:

> There is not sufficient consultation and communication between the various racial groups which make up our population. There is special need that a more effective consultation between the government and leaders accepted by the non-white people of South Africa should be devised (p. 25).

It is important to note that these statements were made by the member churches of the WCC in South Africa which at the time included the three white Dutch Reformed Churches. However, even before the ink was dry on the document, all but one of the DRC representatives had reneged on it and the Verwoerd government was orchestrating a violent denunciation of it. The exception was Ds. C. F. Beyers Naudé.

The WCC realized very early the connection between racism and economic and political exploitation. It recognized that economic pressures on those companies and institutions that practised racism or supported structures and systems of racial oppression could be an important factor in the struggle to end racism. As far back as 1968, the WCC called on churches to 'withdraw investments from institutions that perpetuate racism'. In 1972, the Central Committee urged 'all member

19

churches, Christian agencies and individual Christians outside Southern Africa to use all their influence, including stockholder action and disinvestment, to press corporations to withdraw investments and cease trading with these countries' (p. 46). In 1975 the WCC asked six European banks to stop making loans to the South African government and its agencies and, two years later, called for the imposition of a mandatory and complete arms embargo against South Africa.

The WCC's record of advocacy for peaceful change in South Africa through economic pressure on the South African government is clear, consistent and principled. As the situation in South Africa worsened in 1984–85, the WCC continued to monitor it closely and to take appropriate action. In response to the crisis that had engulfed South Africa in a cauldron of violence, the WCC held two meetings in Harare, Zimbabwe, in 1985 and 1986. In December 1985, Dr Emilio Castro, the WCC General Secretary, called an emergency meeting of church leaders from South Africa and the rest of the world to discuss the volatile situation that had caused the South African government to declare a state of emergency, to detain thousands of people, including many children, and to send troops in to occupy black townships. A total of 85 distinguished church men and women attended the meeting and adopted the Harare Declaration. The Declaration stated, *inter alia*:

> We have come together to seek God's guidance at this time of profound crisis in South Africa. We affirm that the moment of truth (KAIROS) is now, both for South Africa and the world community. The government has no credibility. We call for an end to the State of Emergency, the release of Nelson Mandela and all political prisoners, the lifting of the ban on all banned movements, and the return of exiles. The transfer of power to the majority of the people, based on universal suffrage, is the only lasting solution to the present crisis . . . [and called] on the international community to prevent the extension, the rolling over, or renewal of bank loans to the South African government, banks, corporations and para-state institutions, and to apply immediate and comprehensive sanctions on South Africa.

The Declaration also called on the international community to observe on 16 June 1986 the 10th anniversary of the Soweto uprising in which over 600 students were killed by the South

African Police. In response, the WCC organized a world day of prayer and fasting for South Africa.

In July 1986 the PCR/WCC organized a meeting between international and South African and Namibian Youth in Harare. In a message to the youth of the world, the meeting said:

- In obedience to God's command we have renewed our commitment to work for the total destruction of apartheid;
- We share a measure of responsibility for the continuing human atrocities in South Africa and Namibia;
- We call for comprehensive mandatory sanctions to be applied against the apartheid regime forthwith and we express our anger with the governments of the United States, Great Britain, the Federal Republic of Germany, Japan and others for helping build the apartheid state. If comprehensive mandatory sanctions are not applied, they must take responsibility for the inevitable escalation of bloodshed;
- We urge in particular the international youth from the USA, UK, FRG and Switzerland to campaign and pressurize the banks to stop all financial assistance to the South African regime.

The series of meetings cited above stand as proof of the determination of the WCC to carry out its prophetic witness against the sin of apartheid. The setting up of the ECPG was a recognition of the urgency of the situation in South Africa and showed that the WCC was prepared to do more than denounce apartheid. Actions and not just talk were required in the struggle against apartheid.

3. Meeting the Churches and Christian Councils

The story of the Eminent Church Persons Group (ECPG) and its mission around the world would be incomplete without a brief account of the role that Churches and Christian Councils played in facilitating the ECPG exercise in the countries visited. Christian Councils exerted maximum effort to ensure the success of the mission. This brief account is intended to inform member churches of the WCC of the commitment by national Christian Councils to the struggle for peace and justice in South Africa and the elimination of apartheid. It illustrates the fellowship that exists within the WCC family. This account is a tribute and an expression of deep gratitude to all those who assisted the mission. At short notice these dedicated Christian workers performed miracles. They were asked to make the necessary appointments with heads of government and to accompany the ECPG to the meetings with government leaders. The Councils also made all the arrangements — hotel bookings, transport, press conferences etc. All the ECPG really had to do was reach its destination; thereafter it was welcomed and taken care of.

Bern, Switzerland

In Bern the leaders of the Swiss Protestant Church Federation, Rev. Heinrich Rusterholz (President) and Rev. Sylvia Michel (Departmentsleiterin), accompanied the group when the ECPG met with Ambassador Ruegg. After the meeting, the ECPG attended a reception and then had dinner with representatives of the Swiss Protestant Church Federation. During the dinner, the ECPG explained the purpose of its mission, discussed the situation in South Africa with its hosts, some of whom asked questions about the issues of violence and communism in South Africa, particularly the argument of the Pretoria regime that it will not talk to the ANC until it gives up violence and disassociates itself from the South African Communist Party. The ECPG explained that analysis of the situation in Southern Africa shows that the issue is neither communism nor violence — the issue is the determination of whites to hold on to power. The South African government has negotiated with marxist Angolans and Cubans while its soldiers and theirs were still shooting each other; communism is merely used as a bogey by the South Africans because they know that it appeals to some Western governments which ideologically oppose communism.

From the discussions it became clear that the Swiss Federation of Churches had little influence on their own government. However, the ECPG appealed to the Federation to try to pressurize the Swiss government to impose sanctions on South Africa. Some of the Swiss church people said that in Switzerland they were expected not to mix Christianity or faith with politics. Anyone who advocated sanctions was considered a marxist, they complained.

Paris, France

In France the ECPG met with three church groups, two Protestant and one Catholic. On 17 January the ECPG had dinner with church leaders, representatives of the French Churches' Department of Apostolic Action (DEFAP) and of the Comité Inter-Mouvement d'Aide aux Evacués (CIMADE), as well as with the working group on South Africa of the Federation of Protestant Churches. During the discussions it became clear that the hosts were concerned about the issue of violence in South Africa. There was a lot of discussions on sanctions. Several church men and women expressed concern that sanctions would mostly hurt black people.

On 18 January 1989, the ECPG met with Mr Christian Lechervy of the Catholic Committee against Hunger and for Development (CCFD) which is primarily concerned with development projects in the Third World. Mr Lechervy said that it was very difficult to mobilize public opinion in France on the South African problem. There were no Catholic groups that lobbied the government on the issue. The French Catholic Bishops' Conference had never made a statement on South Africa. Mr Lechervy said that Catholics were generally conservative politically and tended to see the black political struggle in South Africa as led by communists. The view that the anti-apartheid struggle was communist-inspired was held strongly by those churchgoers who fear black power and feel that black leaders would impose a communist dictatorship if they came to power. Mr Lechervy told the Group that there was a great need to educate the French public on what was happening in South Africa.

That same evening the ECPG had a working dinner with DEFAP and representatives of the Evangelical Community of Apostolic Action (CEVAA) which has a long history of involvement in South Africa. As long ago as 1828 Dr John Philip had published a book, *Researches in Africa*, which catalogued the ill-treatment of the Khoi Khoi people in South Africa. It shocked Protestantism in France, and prompted the sending of three missionaries to work in South Africa in the late 1830s. Since then French Protestants have been working in Southern Africa.

CEVAA tries to inform the French public on the question of apartheid, a question on which the French Protestant churches are divided. Besides the argument that liberation will bring about communist domination, others strongly argued against sanctions saying that blacks would suffer most because sanctions would create poverty both in South Africa and in the Frontline States; still others argued that President P. W. Botha had instituted some reforms and that more time was needed to give the reform process a chance to succeed.

London, Great Britain

The ECPG was accompanied by Mr Michael Smart, Divisional

Secretary, International Affairs, of the British Council of Churches when on 20 January 1989 it was welcomed to Lambeth Palace by the Archbishop of Canterbury, the Most Rev. Dr Robert Runcie. He told the Group that he hoped to visit Zimbabwe later in the year to better acquaint himself with the situation in the Frontline States. The Archbishop had in meetings with British government officials raised the issue of apartheid. When Archbishop Tutu visited London he also met Sir Geoffrey Howe, Q.C., the Foreign and Commonwealth Secretary, at Lambeth Palace. According to the Archbishop, the British government did not believe that sanctions would work. Sanctions had failed to resolve the Rhodesian problem, they argued. The Archbishop told the ECPG that the Anglican Church supports targeted sanctions in areas like imports of coal and gold, as well as airline connections. He did not see why the British government did not cut all airlinks with South Africa. The Archbishop said that 'the hopes for a multi-racial society are running out and those who are fighting for it are getting old and losing credibility.'

Dr Runcie explained that the Prime Minister, Mrs Margaret Thatcher, believed in market forces. She contended that, if there were a prosperous middle-class black community in South Africa, somehow a political solution would inevitably emerge leading to the abolition of apartheid. According to the Archbishop, the Prime Minister felt that the question of sanctions was primarily raised by the anti-apartheid movements overseas. The view of the British government was that the majority of blacks in South Africa opposed sanctions and that the membership of Christians in the mainstream churches was smaller than that of the independent black churches, so that the South African Council of Churches and its member churches did not speak for the majority of Christians in South Africa.

The Archbishop noted that, in the case of Rhodesia/Zimbabwe, 'it was said that the black majority was apolitical — they did not support the freedom fighters, but when the chips were down they knew exactly where they stood — the same is and will be true of South Africa.' He said that our plea to the Foreign Secretary, Sir Geoffrey Howe, for comprehensive sanctions was likely to fall on deaf ears, but he assured the Group that Sir Geoffrey would listen to a well-formulated argument. British Foreign policy, Dr Runcie said, is founded on the belief that in human affairs reason will always triumph. The Archbishop concluded his remarks by saying that the Church in the UK has a lot of contact with the government, more than in other countries, but it can hardly claim many victories.

Canon Roger Symons, the Archbishop of Canterbury's Assistant for Inter-Anglican Communion Affairs, informed the ECPG that his Church had written to all banks asking them not to reschedule South African loans due in April 1990. He also informed us, however, that legally the British government cannot and will not tell banks what to do. The meeting ended with a prayer by the Archbishop for the victims of apartheid and for the success of the ECPG mission.

Meeting with representatives of the British Churches at Interchurch House, headquarters of the British Council of Churches

Attending this meeting on 23 January 1989 were the Anglican and Catholic Archbishops of Liverpool who had just returned from South Africa. Issues that arose during the meeting were the division within the British churches on the South African problem; among congregations some supported Mrs Thatcher in her opposition to sanctions, others supported limited sanctions. Some said that they had heard people in South Africa say 'don't cut off money to South Africa for scholarships.' It was suggested that, whatever actions churches take, the 'measures must visibly relate to the ordinary member in the pews.'

Dusseldorf — Cologne, West Germany

The ECPG met with the executive council of the Church of the Rhineland on 25 January 1989. Rev. Schroer told the ECPG that the Church of the Rhineland was trying to raise money to support the PCR. It had cancelled all accounts in banks that did business with South Africa and the Church of the Rhineland has its own bank now.

The ECPG also met with the executive board of the

Evangelische Kirche im Deutschland (EKD) which was holding its annual meeting at the Evangelische Akademie, Mülheim. Also taking part in the meeting were representatives of the Evangelisches Missionswerk (EMW), and of the Association of Protestant Churches and Missions in the Federal Republic of Germany and West Berlin. The ECPG told the EKD that it should try and persuade the West German government to take a moral position and push the EEC to adopt stronger sanctions against South Africa. The Group said that it was part of a world body saying to the EKD we need your prayers as well as specific actions to help bring an end to the apartheid system.

The EKD responded by saying that, according to its analysis of the situation in South Africa, only the churches and trade unions could bring about change. According to the EKD there were two prevailing views in West German churches on South Africa. One was that the situation had deteriorated while the other was that things were improving slowly — the pace being slow because of fear of the white right wing in South Africa. Strong action by churches would play into the hands of the right wing. In October 1988, the EKD had underlined the necessity of taking reasonable measures. Total withdrawal from South Africa was out of the question for the EKD which argued that 'if we retain some economic and political contact, we are in a better position to influence the situation in South Africa.' Some members of the EKD questioned the ECPG contention that every Deutsch mark that goes to South Africa helps sustain the apartheid system. 'Does it not depend on where the mark goes?', they argued. 'We must distinguish between the task of the Church and that of politicians and business people. Sanctions are for politicians. The Church should be an ethical counsellor.'

Tokyo, Japan

The ECPG met with about 45 church leaders at the Tobu Ginza Hotel on 28 January 1989. They were told that the churches in Japan worked very closely with the Japan Anti-Apartheid Committee. The churches' anti-apartheid work consisted mostly of conscientizing the public about the apartheid system.

It was difficult for the churches to meet with government leaders to discuss South Africa.

In March 1987, the 30th General Assembly of the National Christian Council in Japan unanimously had adopted the following resolutions:

i) that the South African government ought to halt the suppression of black people and eliminate apartheid;

ii) that in response to the cries of the black people of South Africa and in seeking with them liberation, the Japanese government should impose economic sanctions against the white supremacist government of South Africa and compel Japanese companies to leave South Africa;

iii) that all churches in Japan should boycott South African products;

iv) that we respond as Christians who confess our sins of complicity in the apartheid system of oppression, that we continue our struggle against existing systems of oppression and discrimination in Japanese society and that we develop a movement that will seek the elimination of apartheid oppression.

Washington, D.C., USA

The National Council of Churches in Christ, USA, arranged several briefings for the ECPG on the attitude of the US Congress and the new Bush administration towards sanctions and the whole Southern African situation. The ECPG was told that press censorship in South Africa had had a tremendous impact on Congress and the American people in general: 'Out of sight, out of mind.' Some Congressmen were saying that sanctions have not worked and that Congress had done a lot for South Africans already. Mandela had been 'released to a comfortable residence.' The Group was told that apartheid was no longer an issue of public debate in Congress or even in the press. South Africa is a hard story to sell unless there is bad news.

At a luncheon for the ECPG on 2 February 1989, the General

Secretary of the NCCC/USA and his staff were joined by four Canadian church leaders who had flown in from Toronto to meet the Group. The Canadian delegation consisted of the Very Rev. Lois Wilson, formerly co-director of the Ecumenical Forum and Moderator of the United Church of Canada, and currently a President of the World Council of Churches, the Rt. Rev. Sangechu Lee, Moderator of the United Church of Canada, the Rt. Rev. Bruce A. Miles, Moderator of the Presbyterian Church in Canada and Mr Gary Kenny, a staff member with the Canadian Council of Churches.

The Canadian church delegation expressed its appreciation of what the ECPG was doing. They had come to Washington to express their solidarity and to tell the Group of some of the things the churches were doing in Canada. The Canadian government was playing a leading role within the Commonwealth to secure stronger sanctions against South Africa. That very week, Mr Joe Clark, the Canadian Foreign Minister, was in Harare meeting with several other Commonwealth ministers on Southern Africa. Canada had just been elected to the Security Council. The Canadians told the ECPG that the churches were doing rather well in trying to implement the Lusaka Statement. They were pressing the government to impose comprehensive mandatory sanctions while they were still discussing whether Canada's diplomatic representation in South Africa should be downgraded.

Despite all these actions, the delegation was disappointed that the volume of Canada's trade with South Africa in 1988 had increased compared to 1987. The Canadians felt that what happened in the United States and the United Kingdom would influence Canada's policy towards sanctions. The ECPG urged the Canadian churches not to reduce pressure on their government because, if Canada reduced her leading role within the Commonwealth, weaker members who want a firm stance would be left isolated.

In the course of its discussions with the ECPG, the Canadian delegation issued two statements. They are reproduced below:

> We, along with the ECPG, call on the Canadian government to reassert its leadership in the Commonwealth as member states attempt to act multilaterally to pressure the South African

government to end apartheid. The best way it can do this is by imposing comprehensive and mandatory sanctions against South Africa now.

The ECPG expressed concern that Canada's role as a leader in the Commonwealth group of nations was 'flagging', and increasingly so since the meeting of the Commonwealth Foreign Ministers in Toronto last August [1988]. In the past Canada has, through both word and deed, 'held the line' against the anti-sanctions bloc led by Great Britain, the ECPG said. To abdicate leadership now would leave weaker Commonwealth member states vulnerable to the influence of Great Britain's anti-sanctions lobby.

It would be 'tragic', the ECPG said, if Canada were to abdicate its leadership in the Commonwealth forum now. Canada's role as a leading proponent of a free, democratic and multi-racial South Africa is 'absolutely essential' and 'critical'. 'Canada has an important unilateral role with multilateral consequences.' However, the Canadian government must continue to demonstrate its solidarity with the oppressed people of South Africa, not only with strong words, but also through decisive and concrete economic measures. Otherwise, we believe that its reputation as a leader among nations opposing apartheid will continue to fade.

We also wish to join the ECPG in calling on the Canadian government to:

* act to prevent Canadian banks from, either directly or indirectly through consortia, helping the South African government refinance its foreign debt;
* grant recognition to the liberation movements of South Africa and Namibia as the authentic voices of the people;
* grant economic and military support (additional support in Canada's case) to the Frontline States to help those countries withstand the effects of South Africa's war of economic destabilization;
* set up national and international mechanisms to monitor those sanctions which have been imposed on South Africa.

Following its meeting, the Canadian delegation stated:

We, along with the ECPG, recognize that comprehensive and mandatory economic sanctions are the only viable means of pressuring the Government of South Africa to negotiate an end to apartheid. Therefore, we join the ECPG in calling upon the Canadian government to impose comprehensive and mandatory sanctions against South Africa now.

We reject Canada's current policy of selective and voluntary sanctions which the ECPG rightfully calls an 'ineffective' and 'inadequate' strategy to bring South Africa to the negotiating table. It is unrealistic for the Canadian government to expect business (which is chiefly motivated by profit rather than a moral concern for justice) to honour the government's call for voluntary sanctions if those sanctions ultimately mean less profit. The fact that Canadian trade with South Africa increased in 1988, in spite of voluntary sanctions, proves just how ineffective the Canadian government's policy of selective and voluntary sanctions has been. If Canadian business is to fully support the liberation aspirations of the oppressed people of South Africa, then the Canadian government must compel them to do so by law. Economic sanctions must be mandatory.

Economic sanctions work. South Africa's signing last December [1988] of the Brazzaville Protocol, obliging it to pull its troops out of Angola and clear the way for Namibian independence, can be directly attributed to the effects of international economic sanctions, which have weakened the South African economy and that country's capacity to carry on military campaigns outside of its borders.

We, along with the ECPG, wish to dismiss the view, propagated by the South African government, that economic sanctions hurt blacks the most, and that black opinion in South Africa is against sanctions. The ECPG pointed out that polls taken by the South African government to measure black opinion on economic sanctions are 'extremely unreliable'. Blacks canvassed in the polls have little choice but to say they don't support sanctions because, under State of Emergency law, it is illegal for them to state otherwise. To state support for sanctions would invite detention and torture.

4. The Swiss Government

Bern, Switzerland

On 16 January 1989, accompanied by Rev. H. Rusterholz and Rev. Sylvia Michel, the ECPG met with Ambassador Ruegg of the Ministry of Foreign Affairs of the Federal Government of Switzerland, accompanied by six assistants. Mr Ruegg apologized for the Foreign Minister's absence, explaining that he had gone to Vienna to attend a disarmament conference.

Rev. Dr Canaan Banana introduced the members of the ECPG and explained the purpose and mission of the Group to the Swiss Government. He said that the ECPG was part of the WCC's continuing effort in the struggle for justice and peace in South Africa. He noted the efforts of other organizations against apartheid — the United Nations, the Non-Aligned Movement, the Organization of African Unity and especially the Commonwealth.

The Commonwealth had in 1985 also set up an Eminent Persons Group which had tried to bring South Africa to the negotiating table with the authentic leaders of the black majority. For six months beginning in January 1986, the Commonwealth Eminent Persons Group had travelled throughout South Africa, talked to President Botha and his cabinet ministers; with church and trade union leaders; with members of the United Democratic Front (UDF), and Nelson Mandela; with the ANC in Lusaka and with the PAC.

It had felt it was making some progress when the South

African government suddenly pulled the carpet from under its feet. While the Group was in Cape Town on 19 May 1986, South African troops attacked Botswana, Zambia and Zimbabwe — all member states of the Commonwealth. These attacks sabotaged and aborted the Commonwealth initiative. Of the attacks the Eminent Persons Group stated: 'it was our unanimous view that the Government's actions had made our task of bringing the parties to the negotiating table immeasurably more difficult' [*Mission to South Africa*, 1986, p. 120]. Furthermore the Commonwealth Group said: 'the Government . . . is in truth not yet prepared to negotiate fundamental changes nor to countenance the creation of genuine democratic structures, nor to face the prospect of the end of white domination and white power in the foreseeable future' [Ibid., pp. 132–33].

Finally, the Commonwealth Group strongly recommended economic sanctions against South Africa, arguing that:

> We are convinced that the South African Government is concerned about the adoption of effective economic measures against it. If it comes to the conclusion that it would always remain protected from such measures, the process of change in South Africa is unlikely to increase in momentum . . . and the descent into violence would be accelerated. In these circumstances, the cost in lives may have to be counted in millions [Ibid., p. 140].

Unless strong measures were taken soon, the Commonwealth Group warned that South Africa would be engulfed in 'the worst bloodbath since the Second World War' [p. 141].

It was to avert such a catastrophe that the World Council of Churches had decided to set up the Eminent Church Persons Group and to send it on an important mission to urge governments to impose mandatory sanctions which the WCC and its many member churches viewed as the last peaceful means for the international community to eradicate apartheid without great loss of life.

Rev. Dr Banana explained that the ECPG was visiting the Swiss Government because the Group believed that Switzerland could play a crucial role in events and developments in South Africa. Swiss banks with investments in South Africa contribute to the suffering of black people. The ECPG hoped that the Swiss would cooperate in putting an end to this suffering through disinvestment and sanctions, as well as by using the occasion for rescheduling loans to put pressure on the minority government in South Africa.

The Ambassador responded by saying that the 22 December 1988 agreement between South Africa, Cuba and Angola (under which Cuban troops would begin withdrawing from Angola, South African troops from southern Angola and Namibia, and South Africa would also begin the process that would lead to the implementation of UN Resolution 435 and the achievement of Namibian independence) shows that South Africa was shifting its policy. The policy shift signalled that South Africa was becoming reasonable and willing to move towards negotiation to solve problems in the region.

In response, the ECPG maintained that South Africa had negotiated with Angola and Cuba not because it had undergone a change of heart but because of a change in the material conditions in south western Africa. The Pretoria regime no longer enjoyed a preponderance of political and military power. The balance of forces had changed the situation, denying the South African government the ability to impose its will on others. The South African Air Force with its aged Mirage jets had lost air superiority over southern Angola, making it impossible to provide air cover for its troops trapped at Cuito Cuanavale. Humiliated, South Africa opted to negotiate in order to avoid further embarrassment.

In the 1970s and early 1980s arrogant South African army commanders had explained their military ventures in Angola as 'picnics'. The parents of dead South African soldiers had begun to wonder what was happening at these picnics when their sons were returning from them in coffins. The reorganized Angolan–Cuban army and air force had made the war costly in terms of white lives. Furthermore the South African treasury could no longer afford to pay for the war in Angola and Namibia. And there was always the international pressure. In fact, after the agreement had been reached in Brazzaville, Mr Pik Botha, the South African Foreign Minister, said as much. He acknowledged that international pressure had played a part in getting his government to agree to negotiations.

The loss of South African air superiority over the skies of

southern Angola was particularly significant because it was the result of the impact, albeit over a long period, of the 1968 United Nations mandatory arms embargo, despite the fact that many Western arms merchants broke the embargo. Even so, military sanctions or the arms embargo finally worked in forcing South Africa to negotiate its withdrawal from southern Angola. Its inability to continue paying for the war (due in most part to the poor economic situation in the country) was also definitely attributable to the present limited economic measures against South Africa. Therefore, the ECPG argued for concentrated international pressure to bring about a change in the balance of forces inside South Africa between the government and the democratic movements that would leave the Pretoria regime no alternative but to go to the negotiating table. The South African government has not undergone a change of heart for, while it was negotiating with Angola and Cuba, it continued its brutal repression at home. President Botha was shaking hands with certain African leaders abroad but refusing to talk with the authentic leaders of the people of South Africa itself. The blacks were experiencing one of the worst periods of repression in memory. Newspapers were banned; news was blacked out; the state of emergency continued. In February 1988, 17 non-violent anti-apartheid organizations were banned; by the end of the year the number had increased to 32. Detentions continued. Khotso and Kanya Houses, the headquarters of South African Council of Churches and South African Catholic Bishops Conference respectively, had been destroyed. At the same time, cross-border raids into neighbouring countries continued.

In response, Ambassador Ruegg said that the Swiss government shared in common with the ECPG the aim to dismantle apartheid. He noted that the Swiss government was one of the world's oldest democracies and had a long tradition of freedom, tolerance and respect for human rights. Mr Ruegg told the ECPG that his government, however, has a good relationship with its South African counterpart. The Swiss government has a long tradition of neutrality and, because of that, was opposed to sanctions since their imposition would violate the principle of neutrality to which the government was deeply committed. Furthermore, because of their neutrality and cordial relationship with the South African regime, the Swiss government believed that it had great leverage on the Botha government. Mr Ruegg said that Switzerland had a certain moral influence on South Africa which was keen to retain Swiss friendship. The Ambassador said that it was important to maintain this relationship since at certain crucial times when there is a major crisis, like the intended execution of the Sharpeville six, the Swiss government can bring its influence to bear on South African government actions.

Mr Ruegg remarked that the South African situation was complex. He was distressed, however, that the situation did not look like it would change soon. He was afraid that sanctions would lead to violence and chaos in the country. He said that 'the Swiss government wants to prevent a real and complete breakdown of all economic structures in South Africa'. Mr Ruegg felt that limited sanctions were not effective. 'Comprehensive mandatory sanctions are more convincing,' he said, 'but their imposition would bring about the opposite of what we all want — chaos, a total breakdown of society, no progressive development. This would have a negative effect on the economies of the Frontline States.' Yet ironically, Mr Ruegg observed: 'Violence is not right — unfortunately mankind has sometimes to go through terrific experiences which lead to the maturing of people, nations and societies.'

The Ambassador also argued that comprehensive, mandatory sanctions would hurt the oppressed Africans more than the white oppressors. Furthermore, sanctions were unenforceable.

The ECPG responded by reminding the Ambassador that *The Economist* of 12 November 1988 had said that South Africa had two major sources of financial support — Switzerland and West Germany. The Group also reminded Mr Ruegg of the South African bank loans worth $11 billion that would fall due in April 1990. This sum was the equivalent of half of South Africa's annual export earnings. If Swiss banks and other European and American banks refused to reschedule the loans, or at least demanded that the loans be rescheduled only on condition the South African government negotiate a new political dispensation with the legitimate leaders of the people, the government would be hard put to accept bankruptcy, which would be the only alternative.

On the issue raised by the Ambassador that Africans would suffer most from the imposition of sanctions through increased unemployment, the Group responded that Africans were already suffering. The Group further maintained that the present widespread black unemployment in the country was due to the inherent structural inadequacy and inefficiency of the apartheid economic system. But, more importantly, the Africans were themselves willing to suffer over the short term if this would lead to the elimination of apartheid in the near future, thus ending their suffering. The aim of sanctions was not to punish anyone; sanctions were a means to persuade the South African government to negotiate.

Would sanctions lead to violence and chaos? The Group argued that the most powerful business people in South Africa would not allow the government to let the economy break down. They would act to force the government to negotiate if the situation looked really difficult with the economy on the brink of collapse. For example when, in 1985, two US banks threatened South Africa with bankruptcy by refusing to renew the loans owed to them, some of the country's top business people travelled to Lusaka to talk with the ANC about the country's political and economic future.

The Group again emphasized that it was not the imposition of mandatory economic sanctions that threatened violence, but the refusal to do so. What other option was there to force the Pretoria regime to the negotiating table? Certainly not the maintenance of the *status quo*. There were two ways to bring about change — violence or the peaceful alternative of sanctions. As Christians the ECPG believed that violent conflict would be a tragedy that would bring death, destruction and suffering to many. This they did not want to see happen. The ECPG warned of the determination of the majority, particularly among the young, to end apartheid by any means possible. There was a growing impatience and militancy among the young which could not be contained for too long unless strong economic measures are taken to bring about negotiations.

The ECPG regretted that the Swiss government was opposed to mandatory sanctions. The Group nevertheless called on the Swiss government to impose certain targeted sanctions which would send a strong political message to the South African government. The Group proposed the following:

i) imposition of arms and oil embargoes;

ii) denying landing facilities to South African Airways;

iii) cutting diplomatic, sports and cultural ties;

iv) denying new bank loans to South Africa;

v) refusal to guarantee credits to the South African government or banks;

vi) no rescheduling of loans;

vii) no new investment in South Africa.

Mr Ruegg again reiterated his government's policy of neutrality and opposition to sanctions. He said that under Swiss law the government could not tell the banks what to do.

The Group responded that the government had definitely intervened on previous occasions with the banks, for example, in asking them to investigate how much money former President Marcos had in Swiss banks, and had even prevented Marcos from withdrawing money from the banks while the investigation was being conducted. The Government had also intervened with the Swiss banks when the scandal of laundering drug money forced a government Minister to resign. It was now clear that the principle of neutrality and non-interference with bank transactions could be departed from when the Swiss government deemed the situation serious and intervention necessary in the national interest.

These cases made clear that the Swiss government would act where it was obvious that a crime had been committed. The ECPG reminded the Ambassador that apartheid had been declared a crime by the international community. Authorities should punish those who commit crimes and not negotiate with them.

Refusal to impose mandatory sanctions helped only to prolong the suffering of the black majority. It was not enough to denounce apartheid, what was needed was action to end that evil system. The South African government was a brutal dictatorship which continually asked the international community to give it more time to solve its problems. Dictators always promise time, for that is all they have to offer the people. But if, because of the failure to take decisive action to end apartheid, we grant more time to the Pretoria regime and as a result more political prisoners on death row are executed, we would all be responsible for their deaths.

Mr Ruegg said that his government supported positive measures like giving scholarships and other financial assistance to blacks in South Africa. The Swiss government was also giving assistance to the Frontline States.

The ECPG welcomed that assistance but positive measures should not be an end in themselves. They should not be used to avoid taking other strong measures like sanctions which the Group believes can effectively assist in bringing about the end of the apartheid system. Limited sanctions were not enough. It was precisely the mildness of the pressure of limited sanctions that is keeping South Africa afloat and prolonging the suffering of the oppressed victims of apartheid.

The Ambassador thanked the Group. He said that its mission was timely. Mr Ruegg said his government, though he remained sceptical of what it could effectively do, would look into the question of the upcoming 1990 South African bank loan rescheduling. He maintained that his government through its strict monitoring mechanism made certain that Swiss companies did not take advantage of sanctions imposed on South Africa by other countries by moving in to replace departing companies. Mr Ruegg assured the ECPG that the Swiss government would not fail to react positively should South Africa's major trading partners take strong economic measures against the Pretoria regime. On two occasions the Ambassador told the group that:

> If all countries' air transport links with South Africa were to be looked into, Switzerland would have to reconsider its position since it would not want to be a loophole in the sanctions imposed by the rest of the world. Switzerland does not exclude the possibility of using other methods of pressure other than the ones we have hitherto used.

The Ambassador welcomed the opportunity to discuss and exchange views on the South African situation with the representatives of the ecumenical movement.

South Africa: The Sanctions Mission

A day later, on 17 January 1989, the ECPG sent the following letter to M. René Felber, Minister of Foreign Affairs in the Swiss government:

Your Excellency,

We welcomed the opportunity for the frank discussions we had with Ambassador Ruegg and your ministerial staff members yesterday. We regret we were unable to meet with you in person, but we support the purpose of your most necessary trip to Vienna at this time. We hope that an opportunity for further discussions will avail itself in the future.

This letter conveys our profound sense of concern over the deepening repression and escalating violence that is taking place in South Africa and the cross-border violence and acts of destabilization that South Africa unleashes against neighbouring independent African States.

For some time now, the WCC has followed events in the sub-region with grave concern. We fear that unless determined action is taken by the international community to end the abhorrent system of apartheid, the whole region will be engulfed in a bloodbath never witnessed in living memory.

We have decided to approach you in the firm belief that you possess both the capacity and means to contribute to a speedy resolution of the Southern African tragedy. We acknowledge and support the position of the Swiss Government in its abhorrence of apartheid. However, it is obvious that international condemnation of apartheid is not enough to end the system. We are convinced that economic sanctions are the last peaceful alternative to bring about fundamental change in South Africa. We call upon your government to impose comprehensive economic sanctions against the South African government.

The world is deeply concerned about the support of the Swiss banks for the South African Government. The role of the banks is crucial at this time in view of the forthcoming rescheduling of the loans to South Africa in 1990. We believe that global attention will be focused upon Switzerland on this matter during the forthcoming year as it has been in the recent cases of the Marcos funds and the laundering of drug money. The Swiss government cannot disavow its responsibility as part of the world community.

We wish to make a passionate plea to you in the name of justice to consider taking economic measures as the only remaining peaceful option to force the South African regime to the negotiating table with the authentic representatives of the majority of the people.

Please find attached a memorandum of our mission outlining specific areas of action. We shall await with great expectation your response to our proposals, indicating to us in what practical ways your government can contribute to world pressure being brought to bear on the South African Government.

Please accept, your Excellency, the assurances of our highest consideration.

Yours sincerely,

Rev. Canaan S. Banana
Elaine Hesse Greif
Dr Lysaneas Maciel

On Behalf of the Eminent Church Persons Group

No response was received to this letter.

5. The French and Belgian Governments

From Switzerland the ECPG divided into two parts; one (Ms Elaine Greif, Dr Lysaneas Maciel, Rev. Frank Chikane and Rev. Bob Scott) went to Brussels to visit the European Community; the other (Rev. Dr Canaan Banana and Dr James Mutambirwa) went to Paris where they were joined by Metropolitan Dr Mar Gregorios.

France

Meeting with M. François Scheer, General Secretary, Quai d'Orsay

On 18 January 1989, accompanied by Rev. Schweitzer of the Reformed Church of France, Rev. Dr Banana, Dr Mar Gregorios and Dr Mutambirwa met with M. François Scheer, General Secretary of the Quai d'Orsay, Ministry of Foreign Affairs. He warmly welcomed the Group and apologized for the fact that the Foreign Minister was unable to meet it personally since he was accompanying President Mitterrand on a state visit to Bulgaria. The ECPG explained that the purpose of the mission was to call upon governments of countries like France that have a high level of economic dealings with South Africa to sever those ties and to impose comprehensive mandatory sanctions on the Pretoria regime. The Group expressed appreciation for the role France plays in the EEC on the South African question.

M. Scheer, who was France's first ambassador to Mozambique, replied that, although France discerned some signs of movement in South Africa, she was nevertheless worried about the grave situation in the region. The South African–Cuban–Angolan agreement, which started the process that will lead to the independence of Namibia, was seen by the government as a hopeful sign that perhaps the situation would improve in the future. M. Scheer told the Group that his government was opposed to comprehensive mandatory sanctions which he argued would hurt blacks in South Africa. France preferred selective sanctions which could have a strong impact on the South African economy.

The Group responded to M. Scheer's remarks by saying that, while it welcomed the agreement in south western Africa between Angola, Cuba and South Africa and the prospect of Namibian independence, the agreement should not be seen as a sign of a change of heart by South Africa. Objective material conditions had changed the balance of forces in the region, leaving South Africa no alternative but to negotiate.

Further, the Group expressed disappointment that the Namibians had not been directly involved in negotiations that affected the future of their country. The Group also expressed concern that the UNTAG (United Nations Transition Assistance Group) peace-keeping force that would oversee the transition process in Namibia was being reduced in numbers and that the budget for the process had also been reduced.

The Group argued that whites in South Africa would suffer from sanctions. Their standard of living would go down. Right now, the weakness of the economy is affecting both the whites and the blacks.

M. Scheer, in reply, commented that because the South African government had been forced to negotiate in south western Africa, it did not necessarily follow that it would or could be forced to negotiate with its own black majority. The situation in South Africa was complex and different. South Africa could always respond to external pressure by maintaining that there should be no outside interference in its internal affairs. M. Scheer further said that: 'the South African situation is not even a colonial problem — the problem was not like other colonial problems.' Therefore the approach that one takes or should take must be well thought out and clearly analysed.

M. Scheer said that the French government preferred to work closely through the EEC. The joint actions of the twelve EEC countries were more effective than the action of any one country. He deplored the fact that some EEC countries were lukewarm in their attitude to economic measures against South Africa. He assured the Group that France was one of the leading advocates within the EEC for adopting stronger measures against South Africa. He promised that his government would continue to play this leading role.

The ECPG appealed to the government to do more. There were areas where France could take unilateral action which could be followed by other countries. To wait for the agreement of all EEC countries would be a very slow process since those countries opposed to stronger measures were likely to continue to drag their feet. Concentrating on achieving consensus played into the hands of those opposed to sanctions. The Group asked the French government:

- to tighten the sanctions it had in place against South Africa;
- to end loans;
- to press the French banks not to reschedule South African loans due in April 1990;
- to end all air transport to and from South Africa;
- not to guarantee credits to South Africa.

M. Scheer replied that his government was doing as much as it could to help end the apartheid system. He said that arms merchants, for instance, have numerous ways to evade the arms embargo, but that France was doing everything possible to check and monitor violations of the embargo. The government was deeply worried about the death penalty in South Africa and had expressed its concern to Pretoria. France was giving aid to blacks in the form of scholarships to study either in South Africa or in France, aid to rural development projects and to many NGOs. The government was helping in the rebuilding of Khanya and Khotso Houses. France refuses to grant visas to South African government officials who want to visit the country. However, the government had made an exception when it allowed the South African Foreign Minister, Pik Botha, and his delegation to attend the recent international conference on chemical weapons because of the importance of the issue.

On the question of loan rescheduling, M. Scheer said that the banks were private institutions and the government could do very little as French law restricted government interference with bank transactions. Even state-owned banks were guaranteed independence of action by law. He agreed, however, that 'perhaps the government should look more closely into the matter of loan rescheduling.' He again emphasized the importance of working through the EEC and trying to work out a common programme with the EEC countries. 'If you push the EEC too hard, you may split the EEC.'

Now that the Angolan and Namibian issues would soon be settled, all eyes, said M. Scheer, would be focused on South Africa. France will continue to condemn apartheid and will continue to work with African countries in tackling the apartheid problem. South Africa must feel the weight of the international opprobrium against apartheid. He said that France did not know what else it could do at the present time — more than it was doing now. He promised that his government would continue to monitor closely developments in South Africa. He felt that the mission of the ECPG was timely and that 'the visit will have some effect on the French government.'

M. Scheer concluded his discussions with the ECPG by saying that 'the WCC has sufficient weight — intervention through this mission is helpful — we will talk with other EEC countries and will mention this WCC approach and discuss your specific points.'

Meeting with M. Jean-Christophe Mitterrand, African Affairs, Office of the President

From the French Foreign Ministry, the ECPG proceeded to the Champs-Elysées to meet with M. Jean-Christophe Mitterrand, son of the French President, who is in charge of African Affairs in the President's office. In his welcome, M. Mitterrand explained that the fact that France had diplomatic relations with South Africa did not mean she supported apartheid.

France, for instance, had diplomatic relations with Chile whose government she deplored as much as South Africa's. M. Mitterrand asked the ECPG for new ideas as to what France could do in the struggle to dismantle apartheid. He stressed that it was important for France to work through the EEC, even though when France worked with EEC countries difficulties were encountered. For instance, while France supported the ban on South African coal, she still received supplies of it through other European countries who simply put a different stamp on the coal before selling it on to France.

The Group suggested that France develop a monitoring mechanism to prevent sanctions-busting by other countries. Once again the Group reiterated the importance of comprehensive mandatory sanctions.

M. Mitterrand said that his government opposed mandatory sanctions, but stressed that the reason was not so much that blacks would suffer. That argument was not emphasized in France. M. Mitterrand added that sanctions would strengthen the right wing in South Africa. For example, in the recent [October 1988] municipal elections, it had increased its strength. This was a source of grave concern to the French government. Furthermore, the recent agreement between Angola, Cuba and South Africa had created a favourable impression in Europe of South Africa where she was now being seen as more reasonable than before.

French trade with South Africa was not that large. There cannot, M. Mitterrand said, be really much achieved by sanctions if a French bank pulled out of South Africa only to be replaced by another European bank. It is for this reason that France places emphasis on a joint EEC approach and prefers to do this in private. France always raised the question of South Africa on the agenda of the seven major industrialized countries. France could look into loan rescheduling, especially at nationalized banks like the Credit Lyonnais.

He felt that the 'present WCC visit was opportune, a good time to reactivate the impetus of activities against South Africa.' He promised that for France, especially in the bicentenary year of the French Revolution, 'it is not only how apartheid is applied — but the very principle of apartheid itself that needs to be addressed.'

Meeting with M. Jacques Desponts, International Affairs, Ministry of Finance

M. Desponts, head of International Affairs, Ministry of Finance, reiterated that on the South African issue France was 'the most active and aggressive' country in the EEC. He told the Group that France prohibited grants to South Africa. Recently the government had refused to guarantee credits by the Credit Lyonnais for South Africa's Mossel Bay project. M. Desponts commented that 'everybody can make speeches against apartheid, but it is actions like this that were effective'. He, however, decried the fact that, while French companies lost out on (and they complained about it) the Mossel Bay project, other European banks had guaranteed credits and benefited from the French action.

On the issue of the rescheduling of South African bank loans due in 1990, M. Desponts said that the private banks were free under the law to do as they pleased. But the nationalized bank was not quite so free. The Director of the Credit Lyonnais had recently been changed. As for the loan rescheduling, it was the Prime Minister who would make the decision and none had been made yet. He commented that active anti-apartheid work among the French people could help put pressure on the banks to reduce or terminate their dealings with South Africa.

As far as the transfer of technology to South Africa was concerned, he suggested that something like the Coordinating Committee's list (COCOM)* could be worked out jointly between the government and others to see how an agreement could be reached to prevent the selling of strategic technology to South Africa. The churches could help here. France could take the initiative in this and seek the cooperation of other EEC countries. He ended his meeting with the ECPG by reassuring it that France would continue its efforts against apartheid and that 'France will use the bicentennial year to make a strong statement of principle against apartheid'.

---

*With the exception of Iceland, all NATO countries plus Japan are members of COCOM which is based in Paris. COCOM (Coordinating Committee) controls the export of strategic commodities to Eastern bloc countries.

Meeting with M. Laurent Fabius, President, National Assembly

M. Laurent Fabius is President of the National Assembly and a former Prime Minister. M. Fabius said that there should be no discussion on the issue of principle concerning apartheid — 'it is terrible, it must be dismantled.' Everybody denounced apartheid. 'Problem — what does one do in practice to dismantle it?' M. Fabius said that when he was Prime Minister, he had had some hesitancy and reservations about comprehensive mandatory sanctions. Arguments like sanctions were difficult to enforce and blacks would be the first to suffer were common. Now M. Fabius fully supported comprehensive mandatory sanctions. A long coversation with Archbishop Tutu had changed his mind and convinced him that 'everything or anything is better than the *status quo*.' M. Fabius said that it was hypocritical of the comfortable rich countries 'to say Africans will suffer, when the Africans themselves say impose sanctions'. Countries should ask themselves how they could make mandatory sanctions work.

For M. Fabius it was not so much the problem of comprehensive mandatory sanctions against South Africa as such, but that of creating a precedent. If you impose sanctions today against one country, who comes next? But apartheid was universally condemned, and everybody agreed that it was a special problem and, as such, it required exceptional methods to deal with it. Another problem with applying mandatory sanctions is that the policies of South Africa's major trading partners were not centrally controlled by governments. If they were, a government could simply issue a binding decree to stop all economic dealings with the pariah apartheid regime. However, as it was, their economies were free, and the government could only depend on non-binding regulatory measures.

The Group asked whether it was not possible for the government to do something to pressure companies to abide by government regulations. M. Fabius replied that companies were legally free to do as they wished. Even heads of companies or corporations that have business dealings with South Africa denounce apartheid. But they do nothing in practice to effectively back up their denunciations. 'Yet,' said M. Fabius, 'it would be difficult for a big company to take actions drastically opposed to the government. What is required or what is necessary is strong and deep convictions of political leaders and others against apartheid — a strong political will on the part of leaders that will influence companies and banks.' Timid reminders of regulatory actions would not achieve this.

M. Fabius noted that French economic ties with South Africa were negligible compared to those of the United States, the United Kingdom, West Germany and Japan.

On the issue of loan rescheduling, he promised to ask the Minister of Finance to see what France could do as a strong gesture in this regard.

In July 1989, France would observe the 200th anniversary of the Great Revolution. As President of the National Assembly, M. Fabius was planning a meeting of parliamentarians from the Francophone countries to commemorate the Revolution. He would place the apartheid issue high on the agenda and use the occasion 'to appeal to the world to say and do something about South Africa.'

Both the Group and M. Fabius decried the rigid press censorship in South Africa which had effectively cut off Western public opinion from news and developments in South Africa. But the censorship had not changed the reality of the situation in South Africa. 'One must acknowledge reality', M. Fabius said, 'but one must not be trapped by it — one must struggle to change reality.' The churches and others must do something about South Africa's press censorship which simply helps to hide the truth.

Here at the French National Assembly in Paris, the ECPG had clearly found one of Western Europe's staunchest opponents of apartheid and a strong and eloquent advocate for the cause of justice and peace in South Africa.

Meeting with M. Philippe Petit, Technical Advisor Foreign Affairs, Office of the Prime Minister

Immediately after the meeting with M. Fabius, Rev. Canaan Banana left for the airport. The plans were for him to rendezvous in London with the Group from Brussels in order to meet with Sir Geoffrey Howe, the British Foreign Secretary. It was therefore only Dr Gregorios and Dr Mutambirwa who met M. Petit.

M. Philippe Petit is Technical Advisor to the Prime Minister on issues of Foreign Affairs. In response to the familiar presentation of the purpose of ECPG's mission, M. Petit made the following observations:

● that the general French impression of South Africa was that the situation was not improving; for example, the 1988 October local elections showed the white electorate shifting to the right in favour of apartheid in some towns;

● he agreed with the ECPG that mandatory sanctions could be effective, but only if they were enforced globally. This is where the problem lies. So the position of the French government was to support selective sanctions by working through the EEC. The goal of French policy was to achieve a common political position within the EEC where France took the lead in fighting the reluctance of other countries to adopt stronger positions. M Petit repeated the official view on bank loans, rescheduling of debts, the bicentennial commemoration of the French Revolution, and the COCOM list.

He concluded by observing that French public opinion was not well informed on Southern Africa. Most French people's interest was confined to the French-speaking African countries. More information on Southern African issues could help influence public opinion and, in turn, banks and corporations. The ECPG replied that it was the duty of the government to remind the banks about ethical standards and of the values of Western civilization, as well as of the gross immorality and evil of apartheid.

Belgium

A small party from the Eminent Church Persons Group travelled to Brussels where it was met by Pastor Martin Beukenhorst, President of the United Protestant Church in

Belgium and briefed by two members of the Belgian anti-apartheid movement.

Over two days Elaine Hesse Greif, Lysaneas Maciel, Frank Chikane and Bob Scott gave a press conference, lunched with an ecumenical group assembled by the European Ecumenical Commission for Church and Society, addressed a meeting of non-governmental organizations and were received at both the Belgian Ministry of Foreign Affairs and the headquarters of the European Community.

Foreign Minister Tindemans had been called to a conference in Vienna and the Group met with his Chef de Cabinet, M. Reyn. He was adamant that the only way for sanctions to be effective was when all twelve Community members had reached a consensus and applied them collectively. 'We do have a Belgian foreign policy,' he said, 'but we believe we must put it into the whole EEC foreign policy.' He accepted that continual pressure must be put on the South African regime: 'We want to bring about change, but we have to be realistic.'

Throughout the interview, he continually defended the policy of not moving until each member state agreed, which the Group interpreted as being willing to allow one voice to dictate to the rest. Each of the Group knew that Great Britain was against sanctions. In effect, M. Reyn was informing them that Belgium would put little energy into the matter. The Group developed the view that the Belgian government was keen to keep open its diplomatic ties with the South African government while seeking to resolve the position of a Belgian woman (Ms Helene Pastoors) then imprisoned in South Africa on political charges.

Following the visits to France and Belgium, the ECPG sent the following letters to the French President, M. François Mitterrand, and the Belgian Foreign Minister, M. Leo Tindemans:

> His Excellency President Mitterrand
> France
>
> Your Excellency,
>
> The Eminent Church Persons Group organized by the World

Council of Churches was privileged to visit France from 17–19 January and to have fruitful conversations on the South African situation with M. Laurent Fabius, M. Jean-Christophe Mitterrand, M. François Scheer, M. Jacques Desponts, M. Daniel Bernard, and M. Philippe Petit. Your Excellency was away in Bulgaria on a state visit, and we did not therefore have the privilege of calling on you. We wish to thank the Government of France for the most encouraging reception and the useful conversations we have had, with a very large measure of agreement.

For some time now, the WCC has followed events in the sub-region with grave concern. We fear that unless determined action is taken by the international community to end the abhorrent system of apatheid the whole region will be engulfed in a bloodbath never witnessed in living memory.

We have decided to approach you in the firm belief that you possess both the capacity and the means to contribute to a speedy resolution of the Southern African tragedy.

We would like to express the hope that France would continue to exercise its outstanding leadership in pursuing the exercise of economic pressure on the South African regime, both bilaterally and multilaterally in the United Nations and in the European Community.

We wish to make a passionate plea to you in the name of justice to consider taking stronger and more effective measures, especially in strictly monitoring the implementation of sanctions and embargoes; and also by influencing French banks not to re-schedule debts. We see this as the only remaining peaceful option to force the South African regime to the negotiating table with the authentic representatives of the majority of the people of South Africa.

Please find attached a document outlining possible areas of action.

We await with great expectation your response to our proposals.

Please accept, Your Excellency, the assurances of our highest consideration.

The French and Belgian Governments

Rev. Canaan Banana
Dr Paulos Mar Gregorios
Dr James Mutambirwa

On behalf of the Eminent Church Persons Group.

M. Tindemans,
Minister of Foreign Affairs,
Ministry for Foreign Affairs,
Brussels.
Belgium,

Dear Foreign Minister,

We welcomed the opportunity to meet and have discussions with your Chef de Cabinet, M. Reyn. We regret we were not able to meet you in person, but we support the purpose that took you to Vienna at that time. We hope that an opportunity for further discussions will be possible in the future.

This letter conveys to you our profound sense of concern over the deepening repression and escalating violence that is taking place in South Africa and the cross-border violence and acts of destabilization that South Africa unleashes against neighbouring independent African states.

For some time now, the World Council of Churches has followed events in the sub-region with grave concern. We fear that unless determined action is taken by the international community to end the abhorrent system of apartheid, the whole region will be engulfed in a bloodbath the like of which has never been witnessed in living memory.

We are writing to you in the firm belief that you possess both the capacity and the means to contribute to a speedy resolution of the South African tragedy. We acknowledge and support the position of the Belgian Government to develop your foreign policy within the context of the European Community. However, it has become clear to us that the waiting for collective action of the Community actually risks losing the opportunity to take timely and effective action.

It is obvious that international condemnation of apartheid is

53

not enough to end the system. We are convinced that economic sanctions are the last peaceful alternative to bring decisive change in South Africa, by forcing the South African Government to the negotiating table with the authentic representatives of the majority of the people.

We therefore call on your Government to impose comprehensive economic sanctions against the South African Government and to do it in the knowledge that it will offer an example within the Community. Your leadership is needed at this time.

Please find attached a Memorandum of our Mission outlining specific areas of action. We wait, with great expectation, your response to our proposals, indicating to us in what practical ways your government can contribute to world pressure being brought to bear on the South African government.

Please, accept, Mr Foreign Minister, the assurances of our highest consideration.

Yours sincerely,

Ms Elaine Hesse Greif
Dr Lysaneas Maciel
The Rev. Frank Chikane

On behalf of the Eminent Church Persons Group

No replies to these letters were received.

6. The British Government

Meeting with the Rt. Hon. Geoffrey Howe, Q.C., M.P., Foreign & Commonwealth Secretary

The original plan was for Rev. Dr Banana to join the Brussels group from Paris for the meeting with Sir Geoffrey Howe at 4 p.m. on 19 January 1989. Rev. Carl Mau was also to have joined the Group after flying into London from New York that morning. But due to atrocious weather in London, the appointment could not take place at that time. Rev. Carl Mau's flight from New York was cancelled; he then flew to the Irish Republic where he was delayed for six hours. He arrived in London after 6 p.m. Rev. Banana was delayed in Paris for several hours. He arrived in London after 4 p.m. Dr Gregorios and Dr Mutambirwa were also delayed for several hours in Paris. They arrived in London after 5 p.m. The Brussels group, due in London at 11 a.m., arrived after 7 p.m. They experienced additional misfortune when their luggage was temporarily lost. The ECPG accepted the inconvenience with much cheerful laughter and concluded that providence had intervened so that the entire Group could meet the British Foreign Secretary.

The meeting with Sir Geoffrey turned out to be interesting indeed. He had graciously agreed to reschedule the meeting for 23 January 1989 at 4 p.m. The Group was accompanied by the Rev. Dr Philip Morgan, General Secretary of the British Council of Churches.

The ECPG explained the purpose of the mission. They told

Sir Geoffrey that the situation in South Africa was explosive and expressed concern that the British government was the leading opponent in the EEC, the United Nations and the Commonwealth of stronger economic measures against South Africa. This attitude created the impression, particularly among the majority of black South Africans, that Her Majesty's Government supported the apartheid regime and gave it the confidence that nothing would be done against it.

It was important, the Group reminded Sir Geoffrey, to consider the findings and conclusions of the Commonwealth Eminent Persons Group as a result of their mission to South Africa. That Group had been set up at the insistence of the British government which had thought that President Botha was serious about wanting to negotiate with black Africans about power sharing. The Commonwealth Eminent Persons Group concluded unequivocally that the South African government was not ready to enter into any meaningful negotiations to fundamentally restructure South African society by ending apartheid and creating a just non-racial democratic society. Their report unreservedly recommended strong economic measures against South Africa. It was their view that the apartheid regime must know that, if it was unwilling to end apartheid, strong sanctions would be imposed against it; the Pretoria government should not believe that it was protected from sanctions. The Commonwealth report warned of dire consequences for all South Africans if change did not come soon. It spoke of the prospect of a bloodbath worse than anything seen since the Second World War.

The ECPG, in its meeting with Sir Geoffrey Howe, also addressed the thorny issue of how fundamental change could come about in South Africa. It rejected the view that market forces could bring about the desired political change. The British government seemed to advocate this view, arguing that the free working of the market system would over time, perhaps three or four decades, create a black middle class large and powerful enough to demand, and somehow achieve, political power in South Africa. How the black middle class would so demand and how political power could be transferred from whites to blacks was not clear. How the demands for power would be different in form and style from the way in which blacks are presently making demands for political power was again not explained.

With the agreement between Cuba, Angola and South Africa over Namibia, some people believed that South Africa was now reasonable, and reason would triumph in the long run leading to a peaceful political solution in South Africa. The ECPG rejected this view. It argued that the victims of apartheid could not wait for the 'long run' needed for reason to triumph and for the economy to produce a black middle class. It was necessary to view the South African situation from the perspective of the oppressed to understand the urgency of the matter. The oppressed want change now and it is the considered opinion of the ECPG that mandatory economic sanctions offer for the international community the only peaceful option to force the South African government to negotiate with the genuine leaders of the black community.

The ECPG concluded by noting that Britain had a long historical connection with South Africa. South Africa's black majority were dismayed by the attitude of Britain, they had an unfavourable view of the British government, seeing it as standing on the side of the white minority regime.

Sir Geoffrey, who had been listening patiently, did not take kindly to the remark that people in South Africa had an unfavourable view of the British government. This led to a heated exchange. He began by saying he wanted it clearly understood that the British government unreservedly repudiated apartheid. 'I refute absolutely that we are close supporters of apartheid.' The Foreign Secretary said that he agreed with the ECPG on the need to put pressure on the South African government and maintained that the British government was exerting pressure in a number of ways. However, Sir Geoffrey did not believe that 'comprehensive mandatory sanctions are best suited to bring about the changes we want in South Africa'. Already the limited sanctions that had been imposed were partly responsible, he argued, for the recent turn to the right in the country. Through the quiet diplomacy of the British Ambassador in Pretoria — and sometimes through the Ambassador's speeches and through the statements and speeches of the Prime Minister — the government did apply pressure on the South African government. He maintained that 'our way was the most likely to bring changes in South Africa'. He again strongly asserted that 'we are not enemies of South African aspirations — it is a baseless proposition that the British government supports apartheid.'

Returning to mandatory sanctions, Sir Geoffrey said that sanctions would hurt the blacks, the very people the government wanted to help. Not all blacks supported sanctions — Chief Gatsha Buthelezi did not support them. The Foreign Secretary quoted a statement from the South African Anglican Synod of Bishops which supported carefully selected and targeted sanctions, and feared ruining the economy. He held that their position was contradictory. He also quoted a statement by Bishop Stanley Mogoba, the Presiding Bishop of the South African Methodist Conference, in which Bishop Mogoba said that it was foolish to view sanctions as the panacea for solving the problems caused by apartheid. The Foreign Secretary also referred to the statement by the South African Catholic Bishops' Conference on the negative effects they felt attached to mandatory sanctions.

On the issue of the rescheduling of South Africa's loans, Sir Geoffrey said that the British government would not intervene to try to influence the banks. 'It is,' he said, 'a market issue — in fact the debt is self-inflicted by the policy of apartheid.' The British government was, behind the scenes, doing all in its power to pressure the South African government to release Mandela. The government had played a big role in the commuting of the death sentences of the Sharpeville six. This, and the agreement between Angola, Cuba and South Africa are partly the work of quiet British diplomacy and are proof that 'some change is on the horizon' in South Africa. Our voice is 'heard not always from the roof tops,' Sir Geoffrey said, 'we do not belong to the Jericho school of diplomacy.'

The ECPG, in reply, commented that they found it ironical that those who opposed sanctions, by claiming that they wanted to prevent Africans from suffering, refused at the same time to take decisive action against the South African government and thereby prolonged the suffering and pain of the people. Their failure to act strengthens the apartheid regime. The Africans know and accept the fact that they will suffer and will have to suffer in the short term if apartheid is to be dismantled. The birth of a new non-racial democratic South Africa dictates that Africans bear the suffering that the imposition of mandatory sanctions will entail. But that pain and suffering is nothing compared to the alternative that the Commonwealth Eminent Persons' Group warned about.

The ECPG also reminded Sir Geoffrey Howe that the British government, when sufficiently outraged as in the cases of the Falklands, Poland, or the Soviet invasion of Afghanistan, did impose sanctions without any debate on whether the peoples of those countries would suffer or not. It did not wait for opinion polls on sanctions from those countries.

Returning to Sir Geoffrey's reference to the South African Anglican Synod of Bishops, the ECPG asked whether the British government would support the selected targeted sanctions that the Synod had proposed. Sir Geoffrey replied in the negative.

The Group regretted the British government's position both on comprehensive sanctions and on the list of targeted sanctions contained in the memorandum the Group had presented to the government. The ECPG said that the black majority in South Africa viewed the British veto in the United Nations Security Council against mandatory sanctions with disappointment, sadness and anger. Meanwhile, the white South African regime felt reassured; it should not be made to feel that it was immune from economic pressure because of the British veto. The ECPG argued that the threat to impose new sanctions, especially by Britain, would force South African bankers and other business people to talk to the South African government, urging it to seek a negotiated settlement to the apartheid problem.

Sir Geoffrey replied that South Africa's determination to withstand pressure, both internal and external, is great and should not be underestimated. He also told the Group that the Commonwealth consensus in favour of sanctions was steadily diminishing. He thanked the Group for the exchange of views.

Meeting with the Rt. Hon. Gerald Kaufman M.P., Shadow Foreign Secretary and Labour M.P.

The ECPG met with the Rt. Hon. Gerald Kaufman, the

opposition Labour Party Shadow Foreign Affairs spokesman.

Mr Kaufman told the ECPG that the Labour Party had a long history of opposition to apartheid. He said that the Party supported comprehensive mandatory sanctions against South Africa. Mr Kaufman regretted the British government's reluctance to join in the strong measures advocated by the Commonwealth. He also regretted that the British government dragged its feet in the EEC. The position of Whitehall was isolating the government from world opinion, particularly in the Commonwealth, as well as British public opinion. The Labour Party and the trade unions used all peaceful and legal means available to reduce trade between the UK and South Africa. 'People's sanctions', where customers refuse to buy South African oranges and other products, have been used effectively.

Following the meeting with Sir Geoffrey Howe, the ECPG wrote to the British Prime Minister, Mrs Margaret Thatcher, along the following lines:

23 January 1989

The Rt. Hon. M. Thatcher, M.P.,
Prime Minister
Great Britain

Your Excellency,

Please allow us, Your Excellency, to express our gratitude that the United Kingdom agrees with the international community in condemning the apartheid minority regime in South Africa as abhorrent, undemocratic and unchristian and a crime against humanity.

The purpose of this letter is to share with you our profound sense of concern over the deepening repression and escalating violence that is taking place in South Africa and the acts of violence and destabilization that South Africa unleashes against neighbouring independent African states.

For some time now, the WCC has followed events in the sub-region with grave concern. We fear that unless determined action is taken by the international community to end the abhorrent system of apartheid the whole region will be engulfed in a bloodbath never before witnessed in living memory.

We have decided to approach you in the firm belief that you possess both the capacity and the means to contribute to a speedy resolution of the Southern African tragedy. Your role in causing the convening of the Lancaster House Constitutional Conference on Rhodesia demonstrated what decisive action can achieve. We have also seen the positive results of the arms embargo and other economic measures in bringing the South African regime to the negotiating tables on the matter of South African aggression against Angola, and on the independence of Namibia.

While recognizing your publicly stated view on the imposition of economic comprehensive and mandatory sanctions, we nevertheless wish to make a passionate plea to you in the name of justice to consider taking strong and effective economic measures in concert with the United Nations, the Commonwealth and the European Community, as the only remaining peaceful option to force the South African regime to the negotiating table with the authentic representatives of the majority of the people.

Please find attached a document outlining possible areas of action.

We shall await with great expectation your response to our proposals.

Please accept, Your Excellency, the assurances of our highest consideration.

Yours sincerely,

> Rev. Canaan Banana
> Rev. Carl H. Mau Jr
> Dr Paulos Mar
>   Gregorios
> Ms Elaine Hesse Greif
> Dr Lysaneas Maciel

Mrs Thatcher responded as follows:

South Africa: The Sanctions Mission

2 February 1989

Dear Mr Canaan Banana,

Thank you for your letter and enclosure of 23 January about the situation in South Africa. I am sorry that the pressure on my diary is such that I was unable to receive you myself. But I know that the Foreign Secretary has meanwhile listened to your views and explained our policy in detail.

Apartheid is contrary to my whole philosophy which is that people should be able to live where they like in their own country, exercise their full democratic rights and advance according to merit, not the colour of their skin. But I oppose punitive sanctions against South Africa because I do not see how you can hope to make things better by making them worse. Sanctions would create immense economic and social hardship among black South Africans and South Africa's neighbouring states without forcing the South African Government to the negotiating table. They would also inevitably add to the internal polarization and violence within South Africa.

Our policy will continue to be to urge the South African Government to dismantle apartheid, release Nelson Mandela and other detainees and enter negotiations with representatives of all racial groups in South Africa about the way ahead. I am sure this is the best way to bring about peaceful change.

Yours sincerely,

Margaret Thatcher

On 8 February 1989, a brief debate occurred in the House of Commons on the ECPG's visit to the British government. Some extracts from that debate are reproduced below:

Mr Allen (Labour Party): To ask the Secretary of State for Foreign and Commonwealth Affairs if he will review the Government's policy towards South Africa in response to the representations made to him by the World Council of Churches delegation led by the Rev. Canaan Banana, the first President of Zimbabwe.

Sir Geoffrey Howe: As I explained to the delegation, our objective remains the replacement of apartheid through peaceful means by a non-racial, representative system of government. We do not believe that punitive sanctions against South Africa would help achieve this.

Mr Allen: Will the Foreign Secretary concede that that answer — like the Government's policy on apartheid — is inappropriate and unacceptable in a developing situation which is getting worse by the day? Does the right hon. and learned Gentleman accept that the World Council of Churches delegation, the most high-powered ever assembled, felt that it had had a poor reception from him? Yesterday, it issued a press release in which it said: 'With the exception of Great Britain, we found a willingness on the part of the governments we visited to listen to the delegation and to consider some form of economic pressure.' When will the Foreign Secretary respond? Who is he prepared to listen to on this issue?

Hon. Members: Not the hon. Gentleman.

Sir Geoffrey Howe: Certainly not the hon. Gentleman. [Interruption] I listened to him with attention but I do not respond to him, because I believe that his advice is misconceived, I listened to him, as I listened for an hour and a quarter to the delegation, I listened attentively and with respect to what it said. It did not, however, in any sense diminish my conviction that the imposition of comprehensive mandatory sanctions would create an economic wasteland and contribute nothing to the ending of apartheid. I drew the delegation's attention to the fact that the Anglican bishops in South Africa have recently called for carefully selected and targeted forms of pressure to be chosen which would 'avoid, as far as possible, the creation of further unemployment.' That formulation drives a coach and horses through the case for punitive sanctions.

Mr John Carlisle (Conservative Party): Will my right hon. and learned Friend accept that many Conservative Members will be delighted that the Foreign Secretary gave a poor reception to members of the World Council of Churches, because many of us are worried and suspicious about where the funds of the

World Council of Churches are going? Does my right hon. and learned Friend accept that much of that money is going to terrorist organizations [Interruption].

Mr Speaker: Order. Hon. Members may not all agree with what is being said, but the hon. Gentleman has a right to say it.

Mr Carlisle: Does my right hon. and learned Friend accept that much of that money is going to terrorist organizations, both inside and outside South Africa? The people who religiously give money every Sunday to church collections should be told the facts.

Sir Geoffrey Howe: I listened to the case being made by the delegation, because it was representative of a wide range of opinion from around the world. I pointed out to it, however, a recent comment by the Reverend Stanley Mogoba, who is a member of the executive committee of the South African Council of Churches. He said: 'those who advocate sanctions as a panacea for all the problems of South Africa have had that myth exploded in their faces.'
I hope that the delegation will reflect long and hard on that message.

7. The Government of the Federal Republic of Germany

Meeting with Mr Hans Dietrich Genscher, Foreign Minister

Dr Beyers Naudé joined the ECPG in Bonn. The EKD's Mr Christopher Kohler, Rev. Rudolf Hinz and Rev. Dr Heinz-Joachim Held, who is also Moderator of the Central Committee of the WCC, Bishop Skoll and Bishop Engelhardt accompanied the ECPG. Rev. Hinz and Dr Held assisted with translation.

The ECPG told Mr Genscher that the setting up of the ECPG was evidence of the realization on the part of the WCC that the situation in South Africa had deteriorated so badly that something had to be done urgently to draw the attention of the world to an impending catastrophe in that country. Christians and the churches could no longer leave this matter to politicians. The ECPG was visiting Bonn to ask the government to impose economic mandatory sanctions against South Africa as the most effective route to the negotiating table. Cutting all economic ties with South Africa would help to achieve justice and peace in that troubled and divided country. The ECPG minced no words: 'Every Deutschmark spent or invested in South Africa helps sustain the apartheid regime and therefore its inhumane and cruel treatment of the Africans, which includes torture, detentions and political executions through the use of the death penalty.' Imposition of comprehensive mandatory sanctions could speed the process of dismantling apartheid.

The ECPG pointed out that the latest trade statistics between

Germany and South Africa in the January 20 issue of the *International Herald Tribune* showed that, if the trend continued, West Germany would overtake Japan as South Africa's biggest trading partner. It reported that:

> Total two-way trade between West Germany and South Africa rose by 35.8% to US$3.15 billion in the eight months to the end of August last year, against US$2.12 billion in the same period of 1987. West Germany's imports from South Africa during the eight month period increased by 30.2% to US$1.06 billion while exports to South Africa increased 38.8% to US$2.08 billion. By contrast Japan's total trade with South Africa declined by 3.5% to US$3.99 billion last year from US$4.12 billion in 1987.

The Group noted that before it introduced sanctions in 1986 the United States had been South Africa's number one trading partner. It was clear that West Germany was taking advantage of US sanctions. An example of West German sanctions-busting was the increased flights by Lufthansa to South Africa and its advertisements in South Africa for direct flights through West Germany to the USA. These are obvious replacements for the previous flights by US airlines (PAN AM) whose flights to South Africa were banned by US sanctions in 1986.

The ECPG argued that, even if the German government opposed mandatory sanctions, it could still bring significant pressure to bear upon the Pretoria government by imposing some specific sanctions outlined in the Group's memorandum. The rescheduling of South Africa's US$11 billion loans due in April 1990 could provide the German government with an important opportunity to put pressure on German banks to refuse to reschedule the loans unless South Africa made a political settlement with the majority of its people.

Mr Genscher replied that the government was encouraged by events in Southern Africa, especially the agreement between South Africa, Cuba and Angola and the prospect of the achievement of independence by Namibia which could have a direct, positive impact on South Africa. Successful coexistence of the races in an independent Namibia could not but positively influence racial relationships in South Africa. However, as far as the situation in South Africa itself was concerned, the government detected little change. Despite all its diplomatic pressure on the Pretoria government, the analysis and conclusion of Bonn was that there was no substantial change in the political situation. The Foreign Minister said that he was unable to recognize any indication from leading white opinion makers across the whole broad political spectrum of white South African politics of a sincere willingness to fundamentally change the apartheid system. He supported the ECPG's demands to release all political prisoners, to unban political organizations, to lift the state of the emergency, to end press censorship and to end apartheid. But, the government opposed mandatory sanctions, although it was adopting other measures to put pressure on South Africa. The Bonn government had adopted EEC measures which in earlier years it had not supported. He himself had been sharply criticized by the South African government when he said that Germans were free to buy, or refuse to buy, South African goods.

The ECPG explained why South Africa had negotiated with Angola and Cuba. The balance of forces had changed and this had left South Africa no alternative but to negotiate. In South Africa the government continues to punish those who advocate for peaceful change. That is what the Delmas Treason Trial was all about. The trial lasted three years and ended with long prison sentences imposed on those people who had been courageous enough to say 'no' to apartheid, 'no' to racial discrimination, 'no' to taxation without representation. Those who had demanded the right to determine how they lived and where they lived were found guilty of treason. That trial is only a small part of what was happening while the South Africans were negotiating with the Angolans and Cubans. Thus, the ECPG feels that there are no signs that President P. W. Botha is contemplating any fundamental change. There is no validity whatsoever in Botha's argument that he must be careful about the pace of his reforms because there is a serious threat to his plans from the right wing. In the main, the white community as a whole is afraid to lose its privileges if and when a majority government takes over. Even among the English-speaking white South Africans, support for Botha is very strong. There are a few white academicians, theologians and students, of course, who show concern about the situation in the country but they have no base among the white community at large. All this means that there is no chance of a change among the whites leading to the end of apartheid.

Apartheid cannot be reformed. It must be dismantled. The peaceful way is to adopt measures that will force the whites to change their minds about apartheid, to recognize that it cannot be reformed, and to realize that for the black majority, there can be no going back, that for them things in South Africa will and can only become normal after the eradication of apartheid. For the ECPG sanctions are the only way forward.

The ECPG regretted that the West German government opposed sanctions and that it could not do more than it was doing through the EEC. Those German companies continuing to trade with South Africa were taking risks with their own long-term economic interests in that country. What is worse they were taking risks on the side of injustice and causing pain to others. To those who say comprehensive mandatory sanctions are risky, the Group said that they are a risk on the side of justice.

Meeting with President Richard Von Weizsaecker

President Von Weizsaecker enthusiastically welcomed the ECPG. He told it that the visit was most timely and expressed the hope that it would wake the German public up to acknowledge the present realities in South Africa. The President promised that he would do all in his power to help the cause of the ECPG.

Members of the ECPG explained the purpose of the mission. The Group expressed disappointment with the latest trade statistics between Germany and South Africa which showed a substantial increase over the previous year. The Group argued that the increase in trade gave comfort to the apartheid regime and was a source of great distress to the struggling victims of apartheid who interpreted it as support for apartheid. It had become very clear to the Group, after visiting Bern, Paris, Brussels and London, that the German government had to take upon itself the responsibility of moral leadership, in the EEC and in the UN, against apartheid. Vigorous leadership was needed at this crucial time. The ECPG asked the German government to assume the mantle of leadership. The Group once again reiterated its conviction as to the efficacy of comprehensive mandatory sanctions to bring down the apartheid system with the least degree of violence. The banning of the anti-apartheid conference in South Africa in September 1988 had special significance for the ECPG. The conference would have brought together all groups opposed to apartheid, including members of the tricameral parliament who were anxious to review the past and discuss new non-violent approaches in the continuing anti-apartheid struggle. The ban literally meant the banning or outlawing of non-violence. What does this mean for the future, if non-violent groups are told that their methods were illegal? Within South Africa the expectations of outside help were high. There is a belief that strong economic pressure from Western Europe, Japan and the United States could help in bringing about peaceful and meaningful change.

President Von Weizsaecker basically agreed with the ECPG's analysis. He, however, wanted to help the Group better understand his country's policies by analysing the German public's perceptions of the situation in South Africa. Because of the diplomatic breakthrough in negotiations between South Africa, Cuba and Angola and the prospect of the independence of Namibia in the near future, there was a general impression that things were or would be improving in Southern Africa. In the region, the South African government had undertaken a series of diplomatic initiatives with several African countries. To the German public, it appeared that Africans who knew better and were closer to the situation were becoming more cooperative with the South African regime. The President stressed the fact that, because of the rigid news censorship in South Africa, the German public did not see South African news on TV, hear on the radio or read in the newspapers about police brutality; the result was the general, albeit misinformed, impression that things were changing or improving.

The President told the ECPG that the government was cooperating with the EEC. However, he pointed out that it was difficult to achieve consensus and to adopt stronger measures within the EEC because there were some governments that were ideologically opposed to and even hindering sanctions. He agreed with the ECPG that South Africa must never be in a position where it need not fear that stronger sanctions would be imposed upon it unless it was willing to dismantle apartheid.

On the question of the German government intervening with the banks to stop the rescheduling of those South African loans due in April 1990, or preventing German companies from trading with South Africa, the President replied that there were no laws in Germany for this. Legally anything can be exported to or imported from anywhere, unless expressly forbidden by law.

The view of many in Germany was that comprehensive mandatory sanctions were not good. They would be seen as a United Nations imposition which would put the power of enforcement in the hands of an international organization. The President said that national governments wanted to remain in control of their own houses. Furthermore, there was an almost unanimous conviction that mandatory sanctions could not be enforced; limited sanctions — yes — perhaps. Dr von Weizsaecker emphasized that insisting on comprehensive mandatory sanctions would hinder the struggle, especially in Germany and Europe. It would re-open the debate about who was for or who was not for comprehensive mandatory sanctions. With it, the old debates would resurface — that (a) sanctions hurt Africans; (b) they do not work; (c) they cannot be enforced. Now at least, there is no debate on sanctions; everybody agrees on the need for some kind of sanctions. What is required is a list of a number of steps that can be taken, or rather a list of selective sanctions that can be imposed. That is where the debate should be. If South Africa continues its intransigence and brutal repression, the list of selective sanctions that will or can be jointly agreed upon will grow.

The President remarked that recently a German trade union, which had just returned from South Africa, said that its aim was to strengthen black trade unions in South Africa to fight apartheid — comprehensive mandatory sanctions would cause unemployment, weaken the unions and undermine the struggle against apartheid.

In response to that remark, the ECPG explained that, as apartheid brutality increases, priorities for workers change. In the morning parents go to work leaving their children in the townships and at schools surrounded by soldiers. When they return from work, in many instances, they do not find their children at home. In anxiety they search police stations, morgues, hospitals. Their children are injured in prison. Sometimes they are indecently and secretly buried by the security forces. Some may have gone underground, and then emerge in exile with the liberation forces. The important concern for the parent becomes: how can this unbearable situation be ended quickly even if it means more suffering in the short term? The question asked of them by their children — why and for whom do you work? — is a more painful dagger than sanctions.

The ECPG asked the President to do something to offset the Pretoria regime's rigid censorship which had cut the German public off from the reality of the situation in South Africa. The Group raised the issue of the possibility of organizing a meeting of major German institutions — government, banking, business, trade unions, and the Church — to discuss South African press censorship and its implications in the struggle against apartheid in Germany. The President promised to consider this.

Meeting with Chancellor Helmut Kohl

Dr Held, Rev. Hinz and Mr Kohler accompanied the ECPG on the visit to Federal Chancellor Helmut Kohl. The Chancellor told the Group that his government strongly opposed apartheid. Mr Kohl said that he had lost all hope that the situation in South Africa would change significantly in the near future. He had personally sent the late Bavarian CDU leader, Frans-Josef Strauss, to South Africa to talk to Mr Botha — to tell him that the hour was late and that Mr Botha should do something to demonstrate that the Pretoria regime intended to abolish apartheid. Mr Strauss was distressed after his talks with President Botha. He returned convinced that Mr Botha had no intention whatsoever of dismantling apartheid. The Chancellor emphasized the fact that Strauss's analysis and judgement of the political situation had been made by a great friend and defender of South Africa's white people.

71

When President Botha and his Foreign Minister Pik Botha attended the Strauss funeral, Chancellor Kohl met them and personally appealed to them to take important steps to change the political system. Again he warned them that the hour was late and something had to be done now. Mr Kohl asked for the release of Mandela. He told both men that they were lucky that there were many Africans who were still talking about non-violence as a means to end apartheid.

The Chancellor, however, opposed comprehensive mandatory sanctions. He was also opposed to violence as a means to bring about change in South Africa. He said that he had told President Botha that the issue of violence should be discussed by the Pretoria government and the ANC at the conference table. Even though he had given up hope that Botha would initiate dialogue with the ANC or take significant steps to resolve the political situation, he expressed the hope that a new South African leader might be amenable to changing the apartheid system. The agreement between South Africa, Angola and Cuba was a glimmer of hope. He asked the ECPG what it thought the implications of Mr Botha's current illness would be.

The ECPG responded by saying that they were saddened by Mr Botha's illness — he had suffered a mild stroke on January 18 — and wished him a speedy and full recovery. The Group doubted, however, that any change of leadership would lead to significant changes in the apartheid system. The problem was not Botha — the problem was the system whose philosophy permeated all levels of thinking and decision-making in the ruling party and the government. A change in the whole ideology and practice, and not in leadership, was what was required if apartheid was to be dismantled.

Again the Group gave its analysis of why South Africa had agreed to negotiate with Angola and Cuba. It argued that the material conditions in south western Africa had created a new balance of forces that had forced South Africa to go to the negotiating table. The ECPG argued that mandatory sanctions would alter the balance of economic and political power in South Africa. That would leave the Pretoria regime no alternative but to negotiate with the authentic leaders of the black majority. Sanctions were the peaceful way out of the explosive crisis that existed in South Africa today. In fact, existing sanctions — the arms embargo and financial and economic measures — had weakened the South African economy, making it impossible for it to continue to finance the war in Angola and Namibia. The ECPG argued that sanctions have worked and can work.

The ECPG regretted that the West German government was opposed to mandatory sanctions. It nevertheless argued for strong, selective targeted measures that could deal critical blows to the South African economy. The Group was distressed that German trade with South Africa had increased. This, the Group said, could be seen as support for apartheid. The German government could also do something about the South African bank loans due for repayment in April 1990. The Group appealed to Chancellor Kohl to take up the moral leadership of the EEC in the struggle against apartheid. 'You are called upon by the world community to assume this leadership,' the ECPG told the Chancellor.

Three years earlier, the Chancellor had told a South African Council of Churches delegation that he would do all he could to bring about negotiations between the South African government and the ANC. What had happened? What were the prospects? How did he see the situation now? Mr Kohl was asked. The Chancellor's reply left the ECPG with the impression that the German government had lost all hope in President Botha.

Dr Kohl told the ECPG that he recognized the urgency of the situation in South Africa and that was why he welcomed the timeliness of the WCC initiative and had agreed to meet with the Group. The Chancellor underlined his statement by talking about his experiences under the Nazis. He was three years old when Hitler came to power. He told the Group that he saw and experienced the war with all its violence and brutality. The Chancellor said that he remembered the terrible starvation of 1947. He remembered American vehicles bringing food to distribute to the hungry. He also remembered what his parents had told him, during the terrible Nazi period, that people must not remain silent and do nothing in the face of great evil. On many occasions he had asked the older generation of the Nazi period, what it had done. Had it looked away? He was determined to do something about the evil apartheid system.

'Apartheid is not a subject I can just put in my file and forget about,' the Chancellor said. He concluded his reminiscences about the Nazi experience by observing that the 20th century which had been called by many the age of enlightenment and progress had witnessed so much suffering. Perhaps the 21st century will be one of peace. He saw possibilities for bringing about change in South Africa. He recognized the obligation and responsibilities of West Germany, as a great industrial power, to the Third World.

The Chancellor promised that his government would continue its quiet diplomacy to demand the release of Mandela and all other political prisoners, and the unbanning of all organizations so that all groups should be allowed to function freely. He had personally made it clear to Mr Botha that he was opposed to the Foreign Funding Bill — a bill that could cut off all foreign assistance to anti-apartheid groups in South Africa and thus literally paralyse internal non-violent opposition to apartheid. The Chancellor had instructed the Foreign and Finance ministries to explore the Foreign Funding Bill with others in the EEC so that they could act jointly on the matter.

When the ECPG told him that Lufthansa was busting US Congress sanctions that prevented US carriers from flying to South Africa, Mr Kohl promised to look into the matter and to do something about it. He said that German companies should not step into the shoes of other countries' companies that have left South Africa. Mr Kohl said that he had told German entrepreneurs that there was no future in investing in South Africa today.

Mr Kohl said that he would press Botha's successor to hold negotiations, in Geneva or anywhere, with all the representatives of the South African people. The alternative to negotiations, he said, would be an unacceptable bloodshed.

He promised to look closely into the issue of growing German–South African trade that the ECPG had raised. The Chancellor said that it was not his government's policy to increase trade with South Africa. On the question of the South African bank loan rescheduling, he said that his government was in a weak legal position since German banks were free, by law, to do what they wished. But he promised to discuss the issue with the banks.

The Chancellor said that his government was doing, and promised to continue to do, all it could within the EEC in the struggle against apartheid. He acknowledged that it was not always easy to get everybody in the EEC to support stronger measures against South Africa. He told the Group that in negotiations with the South Africans the government cannot demand too many things. The Bonn government could not, for instance, demand that all apartheid laws must be repealed at once. His immediate priority was the release of Mandela because of his symbolic importance. Mandela is a figure of great historical significance. His release could change the whole political climate in South Africa — even whites would not be uninfluenced by his release.

The meeting with the Chancellor originally scheduled for 45 minutes had lasted an hour and fifteen minutes.

Meeting with Dr Hans Stercken, Chairman of the Bundestag Foreign Affairs Committee

Dr Stercken — a Roman Catholic — told the ECPG that 'Christians have a moral responsibility to do something about apartheid.' He felt that the South African government was afraid that a multi-racial society could or would successfully function in Namibia. Dr Stercken said that several countries were actually increasing trade with South Africa despite their public statements to the contrary. He was convinced that the Angola/Cuba/South African agreement was not due to the change in the balance of forces in south western Africa, as the ECPG maintained, but was primarily due to the rapprochement between the USA and the USSR. Dr Stercken strongly felt that peace and cooperation between Moscow and Washington were needed if peaceful and successful negotiations were to occur to resolve the South African problem. 'Common pressure from East and West,' he argued, 'can solve the apartheid problem. This was the most effective method.' Dr Stercken said that the South African problem had been on the agenda of the meetings between Mr Gorbachev and Mr Reagan since their meeting in Reykjavik. Dr Stercken strongly opposed comprehensive

75

mandatory sanctions, arguing that sanctions would not create an atmosphere among the South African white leadership conducive to negotiations.

Meeting with Social Democrat Party M.P.s, Mrs Totemeyer and Mr Verhengen

The two Opposition M.P.s expressed strong disappointment with the increase in German trade with South Africa. They said that there was a growing feeling in West Germany that the South African government was, as a result of its agreement with Cuba and Angola for resolving the Namibian situation, becoming reasonable. In South Africa itself, the government had moved Mandela to a house with a swimming pool. The SPD M.P.s said that the government generally felt that the interests of West Germany in South Africa would be best served by a peaceful resolution of the apartheid problem. The SPD had introduced strong sanctions measures in parliament, like no new capital or new technology to South Africa and no marketing of South African goods in Germany. These measures, the M.P.s conceded, had no chance of being adopted. The M.P.s hoped that pressures from the trade unions and the churches would continue since they had a chance of succeeding in the long run. The SPD supported comprehensive mandatory sanctions.

On 26 January 1989, the ECPG wrote to Chancellor Kohl and excerpts from the letter are reproduced below:

His Excellency
Dr Helmut Kohl
Bundeskanzlerampt
Bonn

Your Excellency,

We acknowledge that the Government and people of the Federal Republic of Germany have taken a stand condemning apartheid with abhorrence. However, evidence has shown that international condemnation is not enough to persuade or force the government of South Africa to abolish the system which had been rightly labelled 'a crime against humanity'.

We share with you the deep concern we felt in reading last week that the Federal Republic of Germany is now the chief trading partner with South Africa. This dramatic increase in trade sends a most unfortunate message to South Africa. It gives confidence to the regime in South Africa and could be interpreted as support for apartheid, both within South Africa and by the international community.

We believe that effective and decisive economic measures are the only remaining peaceful option to force the South African regime to the negotiating table with the authentic representatives of the majority of the people.

We are aware that all international attempts to make this happen have failed. We believe the recognition of past fruitless efforts requires new dramatic measures. Very clearly, economic measures are crucial in that regard and the role of the Federal Republic of Germany is vital.

Your Excellency, we are of the opinion that you could send a signal to South Africa if your Government were to introduce decisive economic measures and to press at an international level for the adoption of comprehensive and mandatory sanctions at the United Nations.

After analysing the political dynamics within the European Community and the events in the USA, we are convinced that the Federal Republic of Germany could play a significant and historic role in the effort to change the balance of power within South Africa and leave that Government no alternative but to come to the negotiating table.

It is our understanding that in the past the South African regime has modified its position only when it felt the bite of economic pressure and because of the effect of the arms embargo against them.

The measures to be taken should include

- stopping the re-scheduling of loans, refusing new loans, and halting government-guaranteed trade credits;
- applying the so-called COCOM list to South Africa;
- calling a halt to all airline flights to and from South Africa.

77

Parallel with these actions would be the setting up of comprehensive monitoring mechanisms to ensure the implementation of the measures.

It is our profound hope that the Federal Republic of Germany may play a full part in internationally coordinated measures in the struggle to achieve the aim we can all agree on — the dismantling of the system of apartheid.

Please find attached a Memorandum outlining in more detail the possible areas of action. We shall await, with great expectation, your response to our proposals. Please accept, Your Excellency, the assurances of our highest consideration.

Yours sincerely,

> Rev. Canaan Banana
> Rev. Carl Mau
> Dr Paulos Mar Gregorios
> Ms Elaine Hesse Greif
> Dr Lysaneas Maciel
> Rev. Beyers Naudé

No response was received to this letter.

8. The Japanese Government

Meeting with Mr Takamori Makino, Vice-Minister of Foreign Affairs

The ECPG was accompanied by Rev. Kentaro Takenchi, the Moderator of the National Christian Council in Japan. Mr Takamori Makino expressed appreciation for the work the WCC was doing to eliminate apartheid. Although the Japanese Christian Council had requested top government officials like the Foreign Minister and the Prime Minister to meet the ECPG, Mr Makino did not tell the Group why senior government leaders were unable to meet it. The Vice-Minister of Foreign Affairs told the ECPG that Japan had taken determined action against South Africa. It was the only advanced industrial country without diplomatic relations with South Africa at ambassadorial level. Japan, Mr Makino continued, 'supports humanitarian projects for black South Africans. The Japanese government was also giving financial assistance to the Frontline States. The government had also imposed restrictive measures on trade with South Africa.' Mr Makino emphasized that Japan was pressing its business community to reduce trade with South Africa, and that, as a result of government pressure, Japanese trade with South Africa had declined 3.5% in 1988 compared to 1987.

Replying to Mr Makino's remarks, the ECPG emphasized that Japan's economic ties with South Africa were seen by the majority of black South Africans as support for apartheid. In

1987, Japanese trade with South Africa increased by 20% over the previous year — the increase was one billion US dollars. In 1986, the US had imposed strong sanctions against South Africa. To the rest of the world it was clear that Japan was taking advantage of US sanctions. It was only because of strong complaints by Africans at the United Nations about this increasing trade (by 1987 Japan was the biggest trading partner of South Africa) that the Japanese government had persuaded Japanese entrepreneurs to reduce their trade with South Africa. In 1988 Japanese imports from South Africa did indeed decrease by 3% but exports to South Africa increased by 8%.

The ECPG complained that Japan imported South African gold through Switzerland and the United Kingdom and that this trade was not shown in Japanese statistics as trade with South Africa. Statistical manipulation thus helped to conceal the true extent of Japanese/South African trade. The ECPG also pointed out that, although Japan imposed a ban on pig iron, the ban did not include iron ore or coal. Japan was the biggest importer of South African coal. Japan could buy coal from the US or Europe but South Africa's coal was cheaper due to the brutal exploitation of black coal miners. The ECPG further noted that Japan did not monitor its 1985 measures against the sale of computers to South Africa which could be used by the police or the army against opponents of apartheid. Japan is a member of COCOM which controls and restricts the sale of strategic technology to the Soviet bloc countries. The Group suggested that Japan should consider applying the same restrictions when it sells goods to South Africa that could be used by the government either for military purposes or to assist the police in monitoring and/or torturing apartheid's opponents.

The ECPG asked why the Japan External Trade Organization (JETHRO) office was still operating in South Africa, and why Japan had not ratified the United Nations Convention to Eliminate All Forms of Racial Discrimination and the International Convention on the Suppression and Punishment of the Crime of Apartheid. The Group further asked why the Japanese government accepted or tolerated the classification of its business people in South Africa as 'honorary whites' while 'conducting business in South Africa.' The ECPG appealed to the Japanese government to intervene in the rescheduling of

South African loans due in April 1990. It asked the Japanese government to impose comprehensive mandatory sanctions against the South African government and to set up a monitoring mechanism to ensure that Japanese companies not only complied with government sanctions but did not bust US sanctions.

Mr Makino responded by saying that the Japanese government was encouraged by the agreement on Namibian independence. He said that the government had made allocations in its budget for Namibia and financially supported the United Nations' efforts to solve regional conflicts. The Vice-Minister of Foreign Affairs said that the Japanese government had adopted restrictive administrative guidelines on such items as coal, computers and gold. The government had specifically asked the business community to reduce its trade with South Africa.

The Vice-Minister said that the Japanese government did not have to apologize since most of its critics did not take the yen's dramatic appreciation into account. He continued that, for mandatory sanctions to be effective, international consensus was important. He stressed that consensus in the countries that the ECPG had visited was important if any meaningful action was to be taken jointly. When asked if the Japanese government would enforce sanctions or take new stronger economic measures against South Africa which could make an important dent in the economy, the Vice-Minister said that the Japanese government would be willing to work through international forums to end apartheid.

Luncheon with Mr Takasho Onda, Director General of the Middle East and African Affairs Office

Mr Onda told the ECPG that he had visited South Africa and that he was therefore acquainted with the South African problem. He welcomed the timeliness of the ECPG's visit. The Group in turn gave its analysis of the South African situation. They told Mr Onda that the situation was explosive and that the ECPG had come to Japan to appeal to the government to take decisive action. Because Japan had a high level of trade with

81

South Africa, she had a lever that she could use to persuade the Pretoria regime to negotiate for an end to apartheid with legitimate leaders of the black majority. She could impose comprehensive mandatory sanctions. The Group expressed disappointment that Japan was now South Africa's biggest trading partner and asked why the government operated the JETHRO office in South Africa where it handled trade and other diplomatic relations.

The Director General responded by saying that the Japanese government was restricting trade with South Africa. Mr Onda said a total trade ban against South Africa must be introduced internationally and, if it was introduced, Japan would join the ban. He denied that the JETHRO office promoted trade; it gathered information. Mr Onda said that contact with South Africa was useful as it enabled the Japanese government to apply diplomatic pressure on South Africa. The Director General told the Group that Japan would like to increase trade with the Frontline States. The Group suggested that Japan should consider transferring the JETHRO office to Zambia or Zimbabwe — this would be a great symbolic act that would demonstrate Japan's displeasure with and disapproval of apartheid and show commitment to the Frontline States which South Africa seeks persistently to destabilize.

Mr Onda said that he was aware that many blacks demanded stronger sanctions but he was not convinced that comprehensive mandatory sanctions were the best way to bring about change in South Africa. Japan's economic power was intended to influence the Pretoria regime to change. After all, Mr Onda said, Japan's trade with South Africa was only 0.01% of the country's worldwide trade and therefore it was not that important to Japan. Of the increase in Japanese trade, the Director General argued that most of it was due to the change in the exchange rate of the yen which made the value of South African/Japanese trade very big when calculated in US dollars.

The ECPG argued that trade strengthened South Africa. Ethically and morally, apartheid was evil. Japan must not be seen to be supporting such a system. Apartheid was a unique case which required extraordinary measures to end it.

Mr Onda told the Group that there was no agreement among Western countries and Japan that economic sanctions was the only way to end apartheid. In response to the view that Japan was taking advantage of other countries' sanctions, he said that the government could not order companies to stop trading with South Africa — it could only plead with them.

The Group observed that Mr Onda had on several occasions said that if other governments took stronger action, it would follow their example; it raised the question whether the Japanese government was committed to the elimination of apartheid in principle. What was the policy position of the government on apartheid? What was the level of intention, if there was any? Does the government have any strategy or plan at all to eradicate apartheid?

The Director General replied that Japan did not have a lot of experience with Africa. He asserted that the government was still learning about both South Africa and the whole African situation. That is why the government was not certain exactly what to do and did not know whether comprehensive mandatory sanctions were the best way to deal with the apartheid problem.

The ECPG wanted to know why the Japanese government allowed its citizens who went to South Africa to accept the status of honorary whites. By accepting such status the Japanese were not only accepting discrimination against themselves but they were accepting apartheid. Why would the country with the second strongest economy in the world accept this? Japan would make a strong statement against apartheid if it refused the status of honorary whites for its citizens in South Africa. Japanese business men and women should be refused permission to go to South Africa under such circumstances. They should stop doing business with South Africa.

Mr Onda strongly denied that the Japanese were accorded a status of honorary whites when they went to South Africa. There was an animated discussion on the matter which ended only when the ECPG had to go to its next appointment.

Meeting with Ms Takado Doi, Chairwoman of Japan's Opposition Socialist Party

Ms Takado Doi had talked to Mr Takeshita, the Japanese

Prime Minister, and expressed to him her concern that Japan was now South Africa's biggest trading partner. She said the Prime Minister replied that Japan was committed to a strong anti-apartheid position and that he supported the UN stand against apartheid.

The ECPG told Ms Doi that increased Japanese trade with South Africa undermined US sanctions against that country. The ECPG wanted to know what monitoring mechanisms the Japanese had introduced to check the trade between Japanese companies and South Africa. The ECPG also asked Ms Doi whether Japan would not consider the introduction of a COCOM-like list of restrictions on the export of strategic commodities to South Africa.

Ms Doi said that it was important for the Japanese public to know the reality of apartheid. She also said that on the issue of selling strategic technology to South Africa, there were laws on the statute book that made it illegal to do so and that the Opposition should use these laws to prevent the practice.

At the conclusion of its meetings in Japan, the ECPG wrote the following letter to the Japanese Prime Minister:

Dear Mr Prime Minister

We welcomed the opportunity we had for frank discussions with the Vice-Minister of Foreign Affairs, Mr Takamori Makino and with Mr Onda, Chief of the Middle East and African Bureau. We regretted not being able to meet with you to discuss matters which we consider of urgent importance.

We wish to convey to you our profound sense of concern over the deepening repression and escalating violence and acts of destabilization that South Africa unleashes against neighbouring independent African states.

For some time now, the World Council of Churches has followed events in the sub-region with grave concern. We fear that unless determined action is taken by the international community to end the abhorrent system of apartheid, the whole region will be engulfed in a bloodbath never witnessed in living memory.

We acknowledge that the Government and people of Japan have taken a stand condemning apartheid. However, evidence has shown that international condemnation is not enough to persuade or force the Government of South Africa to abolish the system which has been rightly labelled 'a crime against humanity'.

We are addressing you as one of the major trading partners of South Africa. The dramatic increase in trade which has taken place in recent years sends a most unfortunate message to South Africa. It gives confidence to the regime in South Africa and can be interpreted as support for apartheid. Furthermore, such trade actually strengthens and prolongs apartheid.

We believe that effective and decisive economic measures are the only remaining peaceful option to force the South African regime to the negotiating table with the authentic representatives of the majority of the people.

We are aware that all international attempts to make this happen have failed. We believe that new dramatic measures are needed. Very clearly, economic measures are crucial and the role of Japan in that regard is vital. Indeed, we are convinced that Japan could play a significant and historic role in the effort to change the balance of power within South Africa and leave that Government no alternative but to come to the negotiating table.

We are of the opinion that you could send a powerful signal to South Africa if your Government were to introduce decisive economic measures and to press at an international level for the adoption of comprehensive and mandatory sanctions at the United Nations.

The measures taken should include:

— Applying the so-called COCOM list to South Africa;
— Specific sanctions on strategic minerals such as gold and coal;
— Not taking trade opportunities which have been abandoned by those withdrawing trade from South Africa.

Parallel with these actions would be the setting up of comprehensive monitoring mechanisms to ensure the implementation of these measures.

It is our profound hope that Japan may play a full part in internationally coordinated measures in the struggle to achieve the aim we can all agree upon, namely the dismantling of the system of apartheid.

Please find attached a Memorandum outlining in more detail the possible areas of action. We shall await, with great expectation, your response to our proposals.

Please accept, Mr Prime Minister, the assurances of our highest consideration.

Very sincerely yours,

Rev. Canaan Banana
Rev. Carl Mau
Ms Elaine Hesse Greif
Dr Lysaneas Maciel

No reply was received to this letter.

9. The United States Government

Meeting with Mr James Baker, Secretary of State

Archbishop Desmond Tutu and Dr Lucille Mair joined the Group for this meeting. The ECPG was also accompanied by the Rev. Dr Arie Brouwer, General Secretary of the US National Council of the Churches of Christ.

Mr Baker welcomed the ECPG by saying that it was the second such group he had received in the ten days since the new Bush administration had come into office on 20 January. He said the administration was still new but was 'in a reflective mood with respect to problems in South Africa.' The Secretary of State abhorred apartheid and expressed his outrage at the country's detention laws. He said 'though there might be differences of approach on the use of sanctions in tackling apartheid, the Bush administration agreed with the ECPG on the end result of their efforts — the elimination of apartheid.' Mr Baker admitted that in the past the US government had not made 'vigorous efforts in the multilateral foray to muster international support against apartheid'. Perhaps, he said, it was time that the US did act. The Secretary of State indicated that he did not know how specifically the administration would change US policy towards South Africa, but promised that the Bush administration would do whatever it could to end apartheid, and that its policy would be different from that of the previous administration.

The ECPG congratulated Mr Baker on his appointment and

hoped that he would use his position to effect changes in South Africa. The Group was grateful for the strong words against apartheid Mr Baker had used during his Senate confirmation hearings. The ECPG told the Secretary of State that South Africa was virtually under martial law; black Africans were being brutalized under the state of emergency; opposition to apartheid was being criminalized; the Delmas trial treason verdict, where after a three year trial some opponents of apartheid had been given long prison sentences, was of great concern. Of the treason trial verdict, a US State Department spokesman had said that in any democracy such a trial would never have been held at all. The Group asked: what is the point of non-violence, if rent strikes and other peaceful means are treason?

The people of South Africa were being pushed to adopt desperate measures. SACC and SACBC headquarters had been bombed and throughout the country there were politically motivated assassinations. There were many children in detention. What, asked the ECPG, must the South African government do, that it has not already done, to so outrage the world for it to take decisive targeted economic action to end this evil system? 'Your country's reputation during the "constructive engagement" policy was low in Southern Africa,' the Group added. 'The impression was that for some people profits were more important than people.'

The ECPG continued by arguing that, despite all the talk about reform, nothing fundamentally had changed in South Africa. Forced removals were continuing. People were still being treated as not human. A violent clash was inevitable unless apartheid was dismantled. The ECPG was convinced that comprehensive mandatory sanctions alone could avert a bloodbath, and force the South African government into real negotiations. The United States should take the moral high ground and a position of leadership in the struggle to eliminate apartheid. The US could and should take a leading role in a multilateral approach to solving regional problems like apartheid, South Africa's illegal aggression against the Frontline States, and her illegal occupation of Namibia.

Mr Baker replied by asking the Group what specific proposals they had in mind. The ECPG responded by citing the issue of the South African bank loans due for repayment in April 1990. Mr Baker asked if any US banks were involved and which bank was the leading one responsible for the negotiations. He was told that three US banks were involved (Citibank, Manufacturers Hanover Trust and Morgan Trust). Dr Crocker* told the Secretary that a Swiss bank was the leading bank responsible for the negotiations. Mr Baker promised to look into the issue of loan rescheduling.

The ECPG told Mr Baker that the US administration could tighten the US sanctions already in place by establishing a monitoring mechanism to ensure that US companies observed the sanctions. The US could support the Dellums Bill which proposed tougher sanctions measures against South Africa unless the Pretoria regime made significant progress towards eliminating apartheid. The US could persuade other countries not to bust its own sanctions. Mr Baker agreed that sanctions did not work unless they were comprehensive and multilateral, but he argued that comprehensive sanctions were unenforceable. Multilateral sanctions had a chance, but unilateral sanctions were ineffective 'because there are always some people or some countries willing to make a quick buck.' He further argued that 'up to now, sanctions against South Africa had not worked and as a result, in South Africa, the right wing is getting stronger.' He concluded by saying 'I don't think sanctions work.'

The ECPG responded by saying that US sanctions had been in place for only two years — more time was needed for them to become effective, but even during that time the limited sanctions had had a significant impact on the South African economy. The value of the rand had plummeted and the economy had not been in worse shape since the 1930s. And if sanctions were not effective, what alternative would be effective? Constructive engagement had failed. Ironically, the ECPG had discovered in all the capitals it had visited, with the exception of London, that US sanctions had created a climate of readiness to accept the imposition of stronger sanctions against South Africa. The demonstrations by prominent

---

* Dr Chester Crocker, Assistant Secretary of State for Africa in the Reagan administration, attended the meeting as he was continuing in office pending the appointment of a successor.

Americans, leading even to the arrest of some, at South African consulates in the US showed their determination to suffer with the victims of apartheid. There was a general feeling in the countries already visited, in church and anti-apartheid circles, that, if the US did it, perhaps they could and should also do it. In these countries, except Britain where there is already strong public opinion against the South African government, what was needed was either strong political leadership or strong public opinion to pressure the government.

For South Africans, the tragedy was that US policy assured the South African government that nothing would be done to disrupt the economy. The use of the veto against mandatory sanctions against South Africa in the United Nations Security Council left the Pretoria regime feeling that it was protected. 'If they [the South African government] knew that they could not count or depend on the veto of the US and the UK, the South African government would be shocked into positive action.' That shock would produce movement in the thinking of most whites in the country.

On the issue of the right wing, the ECPG argued that, even though the right was strongly opposed to the Angola–Cuba–South Africa Agreement and Namibian independence, the Botha government did not bat an eyelid when it decided to negotiate. The conditions in south western Africa were such that South Africa had no alternative but to talk. The right wing was never a factor. It was used as a factor only by those looking for excuses not to adopt tough economic measures against South Africa.

Mr Baker said that perhaps the best approach might be a combination of methods — economic sanctions and constructive engagement. He said that the Bush administration was looking for new ideas in seeking a solution to the South African problem. The administration was willing to talk to anybody, including the ANC, in attempts to end apartheid. The Secretary of State reiterated that the administration was still reviewing the whole situation. He further said that the administration could not go it alone, it had to work with Congress and therefore would prefer a bi-partisan solution with the Democrats. He again promised to persuade the banks not to reschedule South Africa's loans, but he reminded the ECPG that legally the US government could not give orders to banks.

The ECPG told Mr Baker that a statement saying to the banks that they should use the rescheduling of the loans in order to end apartheid would be a significant moral statement that would have a great impact on both the black majority and the white minority in South Africa, as well as on the world; what people from the rest of the world were looking for in the US was moral leadership in international affairs.

The meeting which had been scheduled to last 20 to 25 minutes in fact continued for an hour and fifteen minutes.

Meeting with the Congressional Black Caucus

During its stay in Washington, the ECPG visited some members of Congress who had played an important part in passing the 1986 sanctions law against South Africa.

On 2 February 1989 the ECPG, accompanied by Rev. Dr Arie Brouwer, Mr Willis Logan and Rev. Joan Campbell, Director of the US office of the WCC, had breakfast with members of the Black Caucus on Capitol Hill. The Chair of the Caucus, Congressman Ronald Dellums, cordially welcomed the Group. The Group expressed its deep appreciation to Congressman Dellums who had in 1988 proposed a strong sanctions bill which had passed the House but was never voted on in the Senate because the Senate had had to adjourn for the November Presidential and Congressional elections. The Congressman intended to reintroduce the Bill in 1989. The ECPG said that the US as a leader of the West should provide moral leadership in the campaign to remove apartheid which was a blot on the standards of decency expected of governments in the civilized world.

Mr Dellums told the ECPG that the Black Caucus had met the Japanese Ambassador to discuss Japan's sanctions against South Africa. The Caucus planned to meet with President Bush and to ask him to assert leadership within the seven major industrial countries (the United Kingdom, France, West Germany, Italy, Canada and Japan) in the campaign against apartheid. Congressman Dante B. Fascell, Chairman of the House Sub-committee on Foreign Affairs, said that President

Bush was still in the process of formulating his foreign policy. He hoped that someone could meet with the Japanese Prime Minister, who was at that time in the US, to talk about what the Japanese government was doing about sanctions.

Mr Fascell said that, because of the rigid press censorship in South Africa, the police brutality previously seen on US television was now blocked out, and because of this for many Americans there was no longer any sense of urgency in the situation. However, because President Bush wanted the support of black Americans, the Black Caucus should ask him where South Africa was on his agenda.

Congressman Rev. Walter Faunteroy said that he would try to get the churches to write to the Pretoria government and to Congress about the South African situation. In these letters they could list the names, along with photographs, of people in detention. Congressman Dellums suggested that South Africans write articles to US newspapers in an attempt to unblock the South African news black out. Stories about torture and detentions could once again stir the American public.

Meeting with Republican Senators Nancy Kassebaum and Richard Lugar

Senators Nancy Kassebaum and Richard Lugar are two members of the Senate strongly opposed to sanctions. However, they received the ECPG cordially. The ECPG explained the purpose of its visit, emphasizing that the mission had been undertaken because of the worsening situation in South Africa. The WCC felt that it should do something to alert the world to the fact that a violent bloody catastrophe was imminent unless decisive and immediate action was taken to end the apartheid system. Senator Lugar said that he had heard similar views expressed by the Commonwealth Eminent Persons Group. He argued that sanctions were ineffective because some European and Commonwealth companies had replaced US companies when they left South Africa.

Senator Lugar expressed his appreciation for the Group coming to intercede with the US government. He said that it was difficult for the Senate to take the lead in campaigning for sanctions. It was up to President Bush to provide the strong leadership required on this matter. He was willing to query the President as to what he intended to do.

Senator Kassebaum described the visit as timely. She complained that European countries had not adopted sanctions similar to those of the US. She, however, made it clear that she opposed mandatory sanctions — asserting that Frontline States like Zimbabwe would suffer if mandatory sanctions were imposed on South Africa. Senator Lugar said that in 1986 Congress had played an important role in the adoption of US sanctions but today Congress was ambivalent. Both Senators said that they would not support stronger sanctions measures against South Africa.

Ms Kassebaum said that a lot of US television programmes were shown on South African television. She commented that US actors would make a strong statement against South African press censorship if they refused to have their shows played on South African television. Mr Lugar said that the US government needed to work closely and effectively with other European countries, but the country was still waiting for Secretary of State Baker to assert his leadership.

Meeting with Democratic Senators Paul Simon, Alan Cranston and Claiborne Pell

Senator Simon expressed his appreciation for what the ECPG was doing and trying to achieve. Secretary of State Baker had told him of his useful meeting with the ECPG and that the South African problem was one of the most difficult he had to deal with. He said that he wished there was an alternative to sanctions and that he was willing to discuss with Japan and the European countries the possibility of those countries adopting similarly strong sanctions to those the US had imposed on South Africa. Senator Simon felt that Mr Baker would be more open and frank than his predecessor. The Bush administration would be more sensitive on South Africa than the previous Reagan administration.

Senator Simon said that Senators Kennedy, Cranston and himself were going to talk to the Japanese ambassador about

Japan breaking US sanctions. They would also introduce legislation to get the administration to call upon other countries to adopt sanctions similar to those imposed by the US against South Africa. The Senator saw the possibility of the US not using its veto in the Security Council against the imposition of mandatory sanctions against South Africa. Mr Simon said that he would ask the administration to put the South African question on the agenda of meetings of the seven industrialized nations.

The ECPG stressed the need for strong US leadership on the multilateral level; they also suggested the desirability of unilateral action by the US which it could then ask other countries to follow. Senator Simon said that in South Africa there was no disagreement on the impact on the economy made by even the limited US sanctions. He expressed his admiration for the religious community in South Africa which was standing up for the truth — an effort he described as more than just a Sunday sermon. It was necessary and vital action that would eventually and inevitably lead to the dismantling of apartheid.

Senator Cranston, a veteran anti-apartheid campaigner, needed no persuading on sanctions. As its Chairman, Senator Claiborne Pell could be an important influence in getting the Senate Foreign Affairs Committee to take up the issue of sanctions against South Africa.

Meeting with Senator Kennedy

The Group met only briefly with Senator Kennedy who had to leave to vote in the Senate. The Senator promised to continue to work on the South African problem. He would try to get the Dellums Bill passed in the Senate, although it would be an uphill struggle. He would also try to get the Bush administration to pay more attention to the South African situation.

Meeting with Senator George Mitchell, Democratic Majority Leader

The meeting with Senator Mitchell did not actually take place.

Senator Kennedy escorted the ECPG to the room where the Group was to meet him. As the Group passed the Senate chamber, they were shown Senator Mitchell replying to a debate on the Senate floor. However, the Group met briefly with Ms Sarah Sewell, the Senator's specialist on Southern Africa. Ms Sewell listened to the Group as it told her that the US had to give strong moral leadership on the South African issue to the rest of the world. The ECPG also suggested that the US take unilateral action in addition to also playing a multilateral role. The Group asked Ms Sewell to convey to Senator Mitchell that the view expressed by some Americans that US sanctions were not working was incorrect. The truth was that US sanctions had created a climate throughout the world of a readiness to adopt sanctions against South Africa.

After its meetings in Washington, the ECPG wrote to President Bush along the following lines:

Dear Mr President

We congratulate you on your election and inauguration as President of the United States. Your accession to the presidency of this great country comes at an opportune time in the history of the Southern African sub-region. We commend the efforts of the United States in helping resolve the conflict in South Western Africa, which have helped to open the way for the achievement of Namibian independence.

The sanctions the United States Government have imposed on South Africa to date have had some effect but regrettably the internal situation in that country has continued to deteriorate. We call on the United States to provide the international leadership that is so essential at this time. It is imperative that the United States redouble its efforts applying comprehensive sanctions and implementing an internal monitoring system to ensure wide observance of those sanctions, as well as calling on the international community to refrain from undermining them.

The USA is a country which has been founded on democratic principles. As Christians, we believe that we have a duty to do all we can to bring about justice and peace in South Africa.

We enclose a Memorandum that expresses our views on how

95

this can now proceed. We have appreciated the opportunity to discuss this with Secretary of State Baker.

Please accept, Mr President, the assurance of our highest consideration.

Yours sincerely,

Rev. Canaan Banana
Archbishop Desmond Tutu
Dr Paulos Mar Gregorios
Ms Elaine Hesse Greif
Dr Lysaneas Maciel
Rev. Carl Mau
Ms Lucille Mair

10. Meeting International and Other Organizations

The European Economic Community

The ECPG was unable to meet as planned the Commissioner for External Relations, M Andriesson, as he was not available. Instead, it met with his *Chef de Cabinet*, M Wijnmalen and a group of aid, development and African division officials. M Wijnmalen stressed the importance of national policies. He re-affirmed that the twelve member states of the Community were committed to the abolition of apartheid through peaceful means, but that collectively they could do very little. 'The treaties of the European Community do not refer to political actions. It is the member states which must focus on the political.'

The ECPG heard that the European Community had introduced both 'restrictive' and 'positive' measures in regard to South Africa. They were introduced together to provide a balanced approach and because many believed it was unjust to impose punitive measures without, at the same time, trying to support the victims of apartheid. However, in recent years the commitment to 'restrictive measures' had waned and enthusiasm for 'positive measures' (such as aid and diplomatic approaches) increased.

Michel Mallet of the French Anti-Apartheid Movement (AAM)

M Mallet told the Group of his organization's work in France.

The AAM tried to conscientize the French public, whose interest in South Africa was small, about the brutality of the apartheid system. It also played a coordinating role, trying to bring together thirty groups working against apartheid. The AAM campaigned for stronger economic sanctions against South Africa. Between 1985 and 1986 some sanctions had been adopted by the French government. The AAM was now trying to pressure the government to institute a monitoring mechanism to ensure that companies and business people complied with the sanctions that had been adopted.

Meeting with Senior Members of the ANC: Francis Meli, Aziz Pahad and Mendi Msimang

The representatives of the ANC commented that, since the 1985 WCC Harare Declaration and the 1987 Lusaka meeting, churches had been playing a leading role in influencing or changing international public opinion on South Africa. The ANC told the ECPG that oppression was now at its worst in South Africa. The institutionalized violence of the system was now supported by the violence and brutality of the military and vigilantes. Yet despite well orchestrated state violence, the apartheid regime had been unable to solve the crisis engulfing the country.

The ANC said that there was an urgent need to increase pressure on the South African government to force it to make fundamental changes and not to ameliorate apartheid through cosmetic reforms. Unfortunately, said the ANC, lack of concrete actions by South Africa's major trading partners gave confidence to the Pretoria regime that it had nothing to fear. The ANC commented that it had noticed a shift in the position of the government of West Germany. It added that there was a need to develop guidelines in Europe for developing a strategy for putting pressure on South Africa.

The ANC acknowledged that comprehensive mandatory sanctions would cause Africans to suffer but argued that 'no country has achieved freedom without struggle and sacrifice'. The ANC pointed out the contradiction in the arguments that sanctions do not work and that they would hurt the blacks most. If they do not work, how then can they hurt anyone? The truth is that sanctions, if enforced, would work. They would weaken the regime and shorten the life of the apartheid system. Sanctions were a peaceful means that the international community could use to help end apartheid. 'If not economic pressure,' the ANC asked, 'what is the alternative that can be used to pressure the South African government to change?'

Meeting with the British Anti-Apartheid Movement (AAM)

The ECPG met with Mr Bob Hughes, Labour Party M.P. and Chairman of the AAM; Mr Mike Terry, Executive Secretary; and Mr Alan Brooks, Deputy Secretary. Mr Hughes said that it was a great disappointment to the AAM that the British government had not learned much from the history of the achievement of independence in Zimbabwe. At the time, the conventional wisdom was that sanctions had not worked to force Mr Ian Smith to negotiate with the leaders of the Patriotic Front. The AAM Chairman said that studies by US academics had subsequently demonstrated that, despite violations, sanctions against Rhodesia had been most effective. He said that the British government needed constantly to be reminded that it has used sanctions before — against Poland, the Soviet Union and Argentina. It was naive, he argued, to believe that increasing trade with South Africa would lead to change. 'If you believe that more and more trade with South Africa would lead to the withering of apartheid, you are naive enough to believe that the more and more you feed a lion with meat, it will become a vegetarian.'

On state violence in South Africa and the armed resistance by freedom fighters, Mr Hughes said 'this was a sign of great frustration — things will get worse — something must be done to eliminate this frustration.' Mr Hughes said that the AAM supported the armed struggle: 'People have a right to defend themselves from violence which in South Africa originates with the state.'

Mr Hughes said that the ECPG mission was timely. He reminded the Group that its mission was only a part of the steady pressure on the British government which would eventually convince the government to adopt stronger sanctions against South Africa.

Meeting with the Pan-Africanist Congress (PAC)

The PAC representatives, Mr Rodwell Mzotane and Mr Rodney Funeka, welcomed the timely visit of the ECPG to the UK. They explained that the basic problem in South Africa was that the Africans were not included in the 1909 Union of South Africa Act. It was this exclusion from the political and economic process which denied the black majority the right to decide how the country should be governed and the land and wealth distributed that the PAC was fighting against. The PAC representatives emphasized that their organization was not terroristic, but was an organization fighting for freedom whose aim was to create an equilibrium between the contending parties in South Africa and to bring them to the negotiating table: 'The PAC's aim was to destroy the capacity and ability of the South African government to oppress the majority.'

On the question of sanctions — that they hurt the African majority — the PAC representatives said 'our people are dying now. Poverty will not hurt our people as much as bullets would.'

Luncheon Meeting with Chief Emeka Anyaoku and Mr Max Gaylard of the Commonwealth Secretariat

Whilst in London the ECPG paid a visit to the Commonwealth Secretariat where it met Chief Emeka Anyaoku, the Deputy Secretary General, Mr Max Gaylard, and their staff at the Secretariat. Chief Anyaoku had accompanied the Commonwealth Eminent Persons Group on its travels through South Africa as coordinator of the Commonwealth initiative.

The Chief warmly welcomed the ECPG, saying that both the Commonwealth and the ECPG worked for the betterment of humanity. The WCC was playing a major role on such a moral issue as apartheid. The Chief was eager to know how the WCC was following the Lusaka Action Plan, which he highly commended. He explained that the basis of the latest Commonwealth campaign against apartheid derived from the 1985 Okanga statement which stated that all 48 Commonwealth governments, except for the British, believed that sanctions should remain a major instrument against apartheid. These governments were convinced that, unless the Pretoria government was made to feel the weight of international pressure, no significant change would occur in South Africa, and that the policies of destabilization and aggression against its neighbours were intended to keep the Frontline States weak so as to protect apartheid. The idea of successful prosperous neighbours with racial harmony was a challenge to the apartheid system and, therefore, unacceptable. Commonwealth studies had clearly demonstrated the impact that sanctions, or even the mere threat of sanctions, had on the South African government. They showed that not until international finance began to reduce its links with South Africa did the Pretoria regime begin to talk about 'change'. It was also clear that South Africa's period of flexibility coincided with the period of widespread international campaigns for disinvestment and sanctions.

The Commonwealth Eminent Persons Group had reported that the South African government was not ready to negotiate meaningfully for fundamental changes to end the apartheid system. The 1988 local elections were the latest clear proof of that. The elections, largely boycotted by the black majority, were conducted on a racial, and therefore apartheid, basis. The solution to apartheid lay in consultations between the government and the legitimate representatives of the majority. Sanctions could push the Pretoria government to take that direction.

The ECPG found itself in total agreement with the Commonwealth Secretariat.

Meeting with German Anti-Apartheid Groups

The anti-apartheid groups that met the ECPG at Mulheim Academie were mostly church based. Present in the meeting hall were 150 enthusiastic activists — indeed many people who wanted to meet with the ECPG were turned away due to a lack of space. The ECPG was given a rousing standing ovation when it entered the hall. Twelve anti-apartheid groups told the ECPG about their work. Many in welcoming the opportunity to address the ECPG said that this was the first time they had had an opportunity to take part in a meeting of this kind. One participant said that: 'Ecumenical listening and discussing can be enlightening to our churches and encourage them to continue dialogue with solidarity groups. Without the ecumenical movement, we would long cease to be a church.'

The anti-apartheid groups tried to inform and conscientize the public to make up for the lack of news resulting from the Pretoria regime's vigorous press censorship. The groups were working hard with grassroots movements to encourage people's sanctions, i.e., boycotts of South African products sold in German stores. The anti-apartheid groups gave the ECPG much statistical information about West German trade, the exchange of nuclear technology and financial connections with South Africa.

The groups were especially critical of the position of the German Evangelical Churches (EKD) on comprehensive mandatory sanctions against South Africa. They demanded of the EKD that it take a stronger stand on sanctions. The groups also demanded that EKD increase its support for WCC's Programme to Combat Racism. Some groups criticized the EKD for giving separate financial support to the black and white Lutheran Churches in South Africa and Namibia. This they claimed was support for a form of apartheid practised by Lutheran Churches in the region.

Some of the anti-apartheid groups protested against the presence of a South African embassy in Bonn by holding vigils and prayer meetings outside the Embassy. Other groups were campaigning against Lufthansa flights to South Africa which they maintained undermined the US airlines boycott of the Republic. 'Lufthansa,' one participant argued, 'encourages tourism to South Africa — flying over the dead bodies of opponents of apartheid.'

In general, the groups argued that 'economic sanctions are a "must" if apartheid is to be ended with the minimum of bloodshed.' They were convinced of their duty 'to attack the irresponsible actions of the board rooms of the banks.'

The ECPG was impressed by what it described as the positive, creative criticism by the anti-apartheid groups of the positions of the EKD. The ECPG felt that decisive action by the EKD could only be helpful in the struggle for liberation in South Africa.

Meeting with Erns Breit, Chairman of the German Trade Union Congress

Mr Breit had just recently visited South Africa and he welcomed the opportunity to discuss the South African situation with the ECPG. The 7.8 million member German Trade Union Congress had close relations with the two major South African trade union federations, the Congress of South African Trade Unions (COSATU) and the National Council of Trade Unions (NACTU). Mr Breit emphasized that it was important for German trade unions through their support to strengthen black trade unions in South Africa since they were crucial in the struggle against the apartheid system. Mr Breit agreed that comprehensive mandatory sanctions were the most effective way to shorten the life of the apartheid system with minimal bloodshed. He agreed with COSATU and NACTU that 'apartheid cannot be reformed; it must be destroyed — and that a government elected on the basis of one person, one vote must replace the apartheid regime.' The German Trade Union Congress was increasing pressure on the government and the EEC to impose stronger economic measures and was asking for the diplomatic and cultural isolation of South Africa. Mr Breit was critical of the West German government's half-hearted support for EEC measures against South Africa. He maintained that the government should not be seen as a supporter of apartheid and to do this it had radically to change its position towards the South African government.

Mr Breit told the ECPG that the German trade unions had difficulty in refusing to handle South African goods at a port or airport because of legal restrictions. Under the law of compensation, trade unions could be taken to court if they organized boycott actions against South African products by refusing to off-load a ship and were then found to have caused losses to the shipping company.

Mr Breit said that something had to be done to offset the impact on German public opinion of the South African government's press censorship. He concluded his remarks to the ECPG by saying that: 'The German trade unions were doing their best to work with the German churches. But the ECPG has great moral authority — greater than ours — the ECPG has great moral weight to awaken the conscience of those you will meet — don't give them peace.'

Following the meeting, Mr Breit issued a press statement on behalf of the German Trade Union Congress, in which he called for 'stringent economic sanctions against South Africa.' Cited as 'appropriate measures' were a ban on the import of oil, coal and minerals from South Africa, refusing South African Airways landing rights and halting air transport to South Africa. Mr Breit also demanded that no new financial credits be extended in the 1990 debt rescheduling negotiations, that existing German investments in South Africa be withdrawn, and that government guarantees to companies trading with South Africa be ended.

Meeting with the Japanese Anti-Apartheid Committee (JAAC)

The ECPG on its arrival in Tokyo on 27 January 1989 was briefed on anti-apartheid activities at a dinner jointly hosted by the JAAC and the National Christian Council in Japan. The JAAC worked closely with churches and had been involved in the anti-apartheid campaign for twenty-five years. The JAAC informed the ECPG that the South African issue was not at the forefront of Japanese public concern. The JAAC's main focus was to raise public awareness about South Africa by writing and distributing pamphlets on Japanese trade with South Africa. The JAAC informed the ECPG that in 1988 Japan had bought 300 tons of South African gold and 70% of South Africa's platinum, while Japanese imports of maize (corn) from South Africa had increased 14 times in 1986 in comparison to 1985. The maize was used for cattle feed and beer. There was no reason why Japan could not buy maize from Zimbabwe.

Washington Office on Africa (WOA) and Trans Africa

On 31 January 1989, the ECPG met Mr Damu Smith, Executive Director of WOA, and on the next day Mr Randall Robinson of Trans Africa. Both Mr Smith and Mr Robinson told of their organizations' wish to further the cause of justice in South Africa. Their anti-apartheid campaigns included lobbying Congress to enact strong sanctions legislation against South Africa. Trans Africa had organized many demonstrations outside South African consulates in which about 4,000 people participated. The demonstrations and the arrests had played a leading role in influencing Congress to pass the 1986 sanctions legislation against South Africa.

Both Mr Smith and Mr Robinson said that, because of the strict press censorship in South Africa, Americans were not well informed about the situation in South Africa and no longer felt the urgency to do something as they believed that the situation had improved. Americans saw proof of this in the commutation of the death sentences of the Sharpeville six and the agreement in south western Africa. Some in Congress were saying that the 1986 sanctions had not worked since they had not brought about the end of the apartheid system. Americans tended to look for quick solutions and, if they did not get them, then immediately concluded that the proposed solution had not worked.

Meeting with Ms Gay McDougall, Director of the Southern Africa Project, Lawyers Committee for Civil Rights under Law

Ms McDougall's overall analysis of the US perception of the South African situation was similar to that of Messrs Smith and Robinson. Here it is sufficient to note that Ms McDougall's project concentrates on the Namibian situation. However, in relation to anti-apartheid activities, Ms McDougall's group had held hearings in Washington where fifteen South Africans who had suffered detention and torture gave moving testimonies before Congress. Her group also got sympathetic members of Congress to read into the Congressional Record the names of

South Africans in detention. The group attempted to expose how the US government tried to circumvent sanctions and had taken the government to court in an attempt to get it to enforce sanctions.

Meeting with US Anti-Apartheid Groups

The ECPG group met with twelve, mostly church based, anti-apartheid groups in New York City. Here it is not possible to explain what all the different groups did. All had, however, in one way or another, been for a long time involved in the campaign against apartheid. They had been involved in the disinvestment campaign and some were now active in the campaign to boycott the Shell Corporation's products in the US. Some groups worked for people's sanctions in churches and universities, local and state governments. All were working against the rescheduling of South African bank loans due in April 1990. Many of the groups were working to get their churches to adopt and implement the Lusaka Action Plan.

Meeting with Dr Javier Perez de Cuellar, Secretary-General of the United Nations

After listening to a brief report and analysis of the ECPG's visits to the various capitals, Dr de Cuellar assured the Group of his moral and political support for its mission. He also said that he was encouraged by the US willingness to re-evaluate its policies towards Southern Africa and by the views of the West German government on the situation in Southern Africa.

Most of the time with the UN Secretary-General was spent discussing Namibia. The ECPG had raised the Namibian issue and expressed concern over the reduction in the size of the UNTAG force with every government it had met. Dr de Cuellar explained that it was only after a deep and troubled reflection that he had accepted the demand by the permanent members of the Security Council to reduce the UNTAG force. Refusal to accept the reduction would have postponed the process leading to Namibian independence. He had not wanted to accept responsibility for continuing the suffering of the Namibian people. Dr de Cuellar said that he had decided to grasp the opportunity to test South Africa's sincerity. He was now seeking to persuade the permanent members of the Security Council to agree to give him more troops, should the need for them arise. He then went on to give a detailed description of the UN monitoring process in Namibia, one in which he wanted the churches to play a major role. He assured the Group that the churches could approach him for help if they faced any difficulties in being allowed to do so.

On the question of comprehensive mandatory sanctions, Dr de Cuellar said that even if one cannot achieve comprehensive sanctions, attempts should be made to get effective targeted sanctions. He also suggested holding seminars on sanctions in those countries most resistant to stronger economic measures against South Africa. The Secretary-General told the ECPG that limited sanctions had helped achieve progress towards the independence of Namibia. If stronger measures were taken against South Africa, there were great possibilities.

Later that morning the UN Special Committee Against Apartheid held a special session to hear a report on the ECPG mission. The Rev. Dr Banana, Rev. Frank Chikane and Dr L. Mair addressed the Special Committee on behalf of the ECPG. In his address, the Rev. Frank Chikane said the situation in the country was deteriorating. Last year had been one of the worst years of repression, with the churches under continual attack. During the negotiations over south western Africa involving Angola, Cuba and South Africa, the apartheid regime had banned many organizations in South Africa. The message to opponents of apartheid was that the regime would not tolerate any form of non-violent action. It was also made clear that the regime had no intention of giving up on its acts of repression, abandoning apartheid, or entering into any form of negotiations until the situation inside the country forced it to do so.

Total economic sanctions and other pressures now would help bring about change and the creation of a non-racial society in South Africa, he said, adding that the international community had a moral responsibility to put pressure on the regime to end apartheid.

Lucille Mair, former Under Secretary-General of the United

Nations, said the world media should protest vigorously against the censorship imposed by the apartheid regime, and find ways of beating it. World public opinion should be made aware of the worsening situation in South Africa. Referring also to recent developments in south western Africa, she said the regime was forced into those agreements because of the increasingly deteriorating economic conditions inside South Africa.

James V. Gbeho (Ghana), acting Chair of the Special Committee, said the situation in South Africa was growing ever more dangerous. He pointed to an increased presence of South African security forces in black townships as well as increased attacks on those who were challenging the apartheid regime by non-violent means. He pledged the Committee's continued partnership with the World Council of Churches in working for the total abolition of apartheid.

At the end of the Hearing, the Special Committee recorded a minute of high appreciation for the work of the World Council of Churches in general, and of the ECPG in particular.

11. Sanctions: The Case Against

In the preceding pages we have described the debate on sanctions between the ECPG, governments, Christian Councils and churches. Some observations are in order. All governments and church groups condemned apartheid and agreed it must be eliminated. There was disagreement, however, on how that objective should be approached. Even so, there was no major disagreement on the need for some form of sanctions against South Africa, but there was on the question of comprehensive mandatory sanctions. Some governments accepted the need to adopt stronger economic measures; others rejected this route. But all governments opposed the imposition of comprehensive mandatory sanctions. In chapters eleven and twelve we summarize the pros and cons of the case relating to the imposition of stronger and more comprehensive sanctions.

(1) The December 1988 agreement between Angola, Cuba and South Africa opening up the process for Namibia's independence was cited as evidence that the South African government was now reasonable, and had accepted the need to seek negotiated solutions. Reason would eventually triumph and there was a need to give the Pretoria regime a chance. Imposition of stronger sanctions would destroy the goodwill and momentum created by the December 1988 agreement and undermine whatever possibilities there were for progress towards a peaceful resolution of the South African problem. mean it could be forced to do so over South Africa. The South

African government had negotiated over Namibia did not mean it could be forced to do so over South Africa. The South African army was strong enough to enforce the will of the government in the country, and had a great capacity to withstand and even ignore international pressure.

(2) Comprehensive mandatory sanctions would most severely affect black people, the very people the world community was trying to help. Sanctions would throw thousands of black people out of work and many families would suffer.

(3) Sanctions could not be enforced effectively, especially as their effectiveness was always undermined by some country or other, or some entrepreneur eager to make a quick buck!

(4) Sanctions do not work. This view was expressed most often in the UK and US where it was argued the US sanctions had not brought about any positive changes in South Africa. President Botha was still in office and the government had not collapsed. If anything, things were said to be worse as sanctions had caused a move to the right, slowing down the process of reform. Further sanctions would force whites deeper into their *laager*.

(5) In Germany, Switzerland, Britain and Japan, it was argued that their continued diplomatic presence in South Africa was important as it gave them leverage with the Pretoria regime. It was claimed that, due to their influence, President Botha had commuted the death sentences of the Sharpeville six. Even the agreement in south western Africa was, they claimed, due in part to their quiet diplomacy carried out behind closed doors.

(6) Not all blacks in South Africa supported sanctions. Chief Gatsha Buthelezi was cited as an example of an opponent of sanctions. The British government argued that some church leaders, like Bishop Stanley Mogoba, the Presiding Bishop of the South African Methodist Conference, opposed mandatory sanctions. Some German trade unionists maintained that South African trade unions were the most important factor in

the struggle to bring apartheid to an end and that sanctions would weaken these unions and thus undermine their struggle against apartheid.

(7) Several opinion surveys by social researchers showed that the vast majority of the black population opposed sanctions as they felt it would cause them to lose their livelihood.

(8) Sanctions would hurt the Frontline States whose economies are dependent on the South African transport network and its ports. Unemployment in the Frontline States would increase and many people could starve. All this would cause political instability.

(9) The British government argued that it opposed sanctions because they would not help blacks economically. It believed market forces should be allowed to take their own course without outside interference. The unfettered operation of market forces would lead to the creation of a powerful black middle class which would eventually challenge white supremacy and apartheid would wither away. In fact, the British government believed the economic problems the South Africans were experiencing were due to the apartheid system itself and this could only be corrected by market forces. The British government would not intervene in the question of rescheduling South African loans due in April 1990. The market would enable the banks to make commercially wise decisions on the matter.

(10) All the governments visited argued that legally they could not force companies or banks to take action against South Africa. Their free enterprise systems allowed banks and corporations to do as they pleased.

(11) The Swiss and the British governments, in particular, expressed the view that the imposition of comprehensive mandatory sanctions would lead to a complete breakdown of all economic structures. Mandatory sanctions would literally destroy the economy and the result would be untold misery for all and a violent revolution. Such sanctions would bring about

111

the opposite of what all who oppose apartheid wished to see in South Africa — revolutionary chaos and not democracy.

(12) All countries, though they had imposed some sanctions, preferred so-called positive measures, like help to black South African students in the form of scholarships either in South Africa or abroad, assistance to trade unions, legal assistance for those in detention, help to the SACC and SACBC, funding rural and other development projects. They argued that emphasis should be on training and equipping the black majority with the necessary skills to operate and manage the economy.

(13) The Swiss government opposed sanctions because they would be contrary to its long upheld policy of neutrality under which Switzerland did not intervene in the internal affairs of other countries, no matter how reprehensible their political system was. In regard to South Africa, Swiss neutrality strengthened Swiss leverage on the government because whatever advice the Swiss government gave South Africa was seen as having no ulterior motives.

(14) The French, Swiss, Japanese and German governments expressed the view that for comprehensive mandatory sanctions to be effective an international body to enforce, monitor and punish violators was required. But this would involve an unacceptable loss of national sovereignty.

(15) Some leaders of the German church group, EKD, argued that the church should not be involved in politics. Instead the church should act as an ethical counsellor in political affairs. Sanctions, they argued, were the business of politicians.

12. Sanctions: The Case For

In contradistinction to the arguments cited in chapter eleven, the ECPG here presents a summary of the arguments it advanced for the imposition of comprehensive mandatory sanctions:

(1) The South African government negotiated with Angola and Cuba not because it wanted to be seen to be reasonable or because it had undergone a change of heart about apartheid. Rather, it was forced to the negotiating table by a constellation of factors. First, the South African Air Force had lost air superiority over the skies of southern Angola and was unable to provide the air cover to enable its trapped troops at Cuito Cuanavale to withdraw without catastrophic losses. Ironically, it was the UN mandatory arms embargo (i.e., sanctions) which had caused a shortage of spare parts for South Africa's ageing aircraft and their consequent loss of air superiority. This was proof that sanctions could work if applied diligently and with determination.

Second, the war in Angola and Namibia had become too costly and, because of South Africa's dire economic situation, Pretoria was no longer able to finance these military adventures. The adverse economic position of the country was again partly due to the limited economic sanctions imposed by the international community.

Even while Pretoria was negotiating over Namibia, blacks in South Africa were experiencing intensified repression. By the

113

end of 1988, 32 non-violent anti-apartheid organizations had been banned and the movement of many people severely restricted. Press censorship and the state of emergency were being more vigorously enforced. Some newspapers had been banned for up to three months. Khotso House had been bombed and Khanya House gutted by fire. Clearly the South Africa government had not undergone any change of heart. It was using brutal methods to keep power in white hands. Stronger sanctions against the Pretoria regime were required to change the political balance of forces within South Africa as a means to force the government to negotiate with the authentic leaders of the black majority.

(2) Blacks are already suffering in South Africa. They accept that stronger sanctions would increase their suffering but they are willing to accept such suffering in the short term if that will lead to the dismantling of apartheid. Already there is widespread unemployment among blacks and sanctions would not greatly increase the numbers of the unemployed. The large black unemployment figures are due to the inefficiency and structural defects of the apartheid economic system. For countries that trade with South Africa and benefit from it to show concern for black suffering if sanctions are imposed is hypocritical. It is patronizing and racist because such statements or sentiments assume that blacks do not understand their true situation and cannot make correct decisions. The main point is that the majority of blacks have themselves called for sanctions.

When in the past London has been sufficiently outraged by the political actions of other countries, as was the case in the Falklands/Malvinas, over the Soviet Union's invasion of Afghanistan or the ban by Poland of the Solidarity trade union, the British government, without even any debate about whether the majority of the people in those countries would suffer or not, imposed sanctions measures. Nor, must one add, did the British government wait for opinion polls indicating the views of the people concerned on the effect of sanctions on their lives. The question has to be asked: is the British government sufficiently outraged about apartheid to act as strongly as it did against the above-mentioned countries?

(3) Where sanctions have not worked effectively it has been because they were neither comprehensive, mandatory nor properly applied. The right wing should not be seen as a major deterrent factor. When President Botha negotiated the withdrawal of South African troops from Namibia and Angola, he ignored the objections of the right. This so-called threat from the right is only used when it is expedient. It has become another excuse for doing nothing. Western nations should beware that they do not end up as apologists for the regime because they wish to protect it from right-wing elements. In any case, the right wing in South Africa may have peaked.

(4) When it comes to making fundamental changes in the apartheid system, the South African government listens to no one. Chancellor Kohl has said that dialogue with the Bothas had led nowhere. All the governments visited by the ECPG had called for the release of Nelson Mandela but the Pretoria regime had turned a deaf ear to their request.

(5) Rev. Frank Chikane, General Secretary of the South African Council of Churches, has called for comprehensive mandatory sanctions as have church leaders like Archbishop Desmond Tutu, Rev. Allan Boesak and Rev. Beyers Naudé, to mention only a few. The two major trade union confederations — the Congress of South African Trade Unions and the National Council of Trade Unions — have called for mandatory sanctions after full debate among their members as to the consequences. The two liberation movements — the ANC and the PAC — have also called for comprehensive mandatory sanctions. Chief Buthelezi opposes sanctions but he represents only a small part of the South African people. If one wants the truth about what black leaders really think, the South African government should release the authentic black leaders from prison and detention and withdraw the law that makes it a criminal offence to advocate sanctions.

(6) With regard to opinion surveys, examples can be cited of polls which have produced different findings to those quoted by the opponents of sanctions. But a number of caveats need to be noted in regard to these polls on sanctions. First, it is illegal in

South Africa to express support for sanctions. Can one really expect ordinary people to take the risk of coming out in favour of sanctions when confronted by unknown pollsters? Is it not safer or tactically more astute to play safe? Also, one needs to be aware of the biases often built in to the pollster's questions. For example, if a worker is told he will lose his job if sanctions are enforced, he is unlikely to express unreserved support for sanctions.

(7) The leaders of the Frontline States acknowledge that their people will suffer as a result of comprehensive mandatory sanctions. Nonetheless, most of them support sanctions because they would shorten the life span of the apartheid regime and end the suffering of their people sooner. As long as apartheid continues, suffering in the Frontline States will be prolonged; they will continue to experience the aggression and destabilization which has shattered their economies. They will continue to have to divert funds from urgently needed services like health, education and other development projects to defence and security.

(8) The ECPG does not accept the argument as to the ability of market forces to end apartheid. Even if it did, it would, as the British government admits, take two to three decades for these forces to produce a 'strong black middle class'. But how, in any case, will such a class topple apartheid? What methods will it use that are different from those used by anti-apartheid compaigners now? It is important in this discussion to view the present situation from the perspective of the victims of apartheid. Why should they be expected to wait another two or three decades? Enough is enough, they are saying, and they have already waited a long time.

(9) The apartheid system is contrary to the principles of Christianity and what the South African government stands for is anathema to the principles of Western civilization. The South African system is a unique case based on colour discrimination. As such, it is justified to demand extraordinary measures, like comprehensive mandatory sanctions, to destroy this evil system.

(10) The imposition of sanctions is not punitive. It is intended to prod the South African government to the negotiating table. Sanctions would not lead to revolutionary violence and chaos. Nobody wants that — neither the non-violent, anti-apartheid, democratic forces, the churches, nor the liberation movements. In fact, business people in the country would not allow the economy to break down. They would force the government to seek a political solution. When in 1985 US banks threatened South Africa with bankruptcy, top South African business people, academicians, students, sports and church people started a dialogue with the ANC.

(11) The ECPG welcomes 'positive measures' but its view is that governments must not see them as an end in themselves. Positive measures are good but they will not of themselves end apartheid. Essentially what they do, in the absence of strong sanctions or restrictive measures, is produce well-educated and skilled blacks who remain oppressed without the power to decide where to live, how much to pay in taxes, who governs them, or even where they can be buried. Many blacks in South Africa see positive measures as an attempt to buy them off, or as a substitute for meaningful and effective measures.

(12) Apartheid has been declared by the World Council of Churches and other church organizations as a sin against God and humankind. God does not compromise with sin. God is not neutral with sin. The sinner must confess and change his ways. The United Nations has declared apartheid a crime. Governments should not thus be neutral to this crime. They should not negotiate with criminals. They should punish them. Switzerland claims to be neutral and so unable to interfere in the affairs of other countries, or in the dealings of Swiss corporations and banks. But recently the Philippines government asked Switzerland to return assets which former President Marcos had deposited in Swiss banks. The Swiss government asked its banks to investigate fully how much Marcos had in Swiss banks and the circumstances under which the money had been brought to Switzerland. The government even instructed the banks not to allow Marcos to withdraw assets he had in Swiss banks pending a full investigation by the government. Recently,

117

there had been a scandal involving a top Swiss cabinet officer accused of laundering drug money into the country. The minister was forced to resign and the government called for a full investigation. In the light of these examples of government intervention, can the Swiss government honestly claim its neutrality demands a 'hands-off' posture vis-à-vis the country's banks. The Swiss government could act if it felt that the South African situation warranted serious attention.

(13) How can the Church be an ethical counsellor in political affairs without involving itself in making judgements on political developments? The ECPG's view is that it is a Christian imperative that the Church should side with the poor — to feed the hungry, to clothe the naked, to visit and comfort those in prison. The WCC has always called upon member churches 'to take a firm and vigorous stand against flagrant violations of human rights through discrimination on grounds of race, colour, culture or political conviction'.

Finally, it should be noted that the South African government, while opposing international sanctions against itself, has not hesitated to use them against its neighbours. It did so even against the Smith regime by threatening to cut off oil supplies to Rhodesia if Smith did not agree to Henry Kissinger's plans to end the Rhodesian rebellion. In 1986, South Africa engineered the fall of Chief Leabua Jonathan's government in Lesotho, one which sympathized with the ANC, through an economic blockade. From time to time, Botswana has been subjected to delays of goods being imported into the country. Zimbabwe has often been threatened with sanctions by the Botha regime. In 1980–81, the South African government, by threatening to cut the number of railway trucks and the flow of oil to Zimbabwe, forced the government of Zimbabwe to negotiate with Pretoria.

13. Reflections

The ECPG talked to scores of individuals in the countries it visited. From these discussions, conducted always with courtesy and respect, a number of distinct impressions emerged. Amongst these was a confused and hypocritical attitude to the use of violence in South Africa, one which amounted to a double standard; as well as an exaggeration of the reputed radicalism (the 'communist bogey') of groups opposed to apartheid, which in actuality expressed an ideological fear for the future of free market capitalism in South Africa. Overall, however, one impression stood out more than any other — behind the reluctance to take decisive action against apartheid in South Africa lay the power of persistent racism in the societies of Western Europe, North America and Japan. In this chapter these attitudes are spelt out in some detail.

Racism

Slavery used to be justified because it served the economic interests of the white races. If their Christian consciences were sometimes troubled about the inhuman way in which black slaves were treated, a resort to the notion that blacks were sub-human and therefore undeserving of humane treatment gave solace and salved their consciences. It was this same general notion that blacks were racially inferior that was used to justify European colonialism with its imperialist oppression and exploitation of Africa in the 19th century. These notions and attitudes still persist. Some of the politicians we talked to implied that blacks required the continued tutelage of whites before power could be transferred to them.

The ECPG heard references to Judaeo-Christian values, for the defence of which, it was claimed, the white Christian West stood. The ECPG got the impression that many whites in the West believed they had a God-given responsibility to keep power from blacks until the latter were 'mature' enough to uphold these values of Western Christian civilization.

Many of those the ECPG talked to expressed 'abhorrence' of apartheid, but they seemed to abhor even more the idea of putting effective pressure on South African whites in order to get apartheid dismantled. The ECPG gained the view that this would have been quite different if a black minority of about five million were oppressing a white majority of about 30 million. In that situation, all the moral and military fervour of the West would have been used to dismantle such a system.

Japan was not involved in the slave trade and the colonization of Africa, as were the European nations. Yet Japanese society exhibits clear signs of racism directed against the Buraku, the Ainu, Okinawans and the Koreans within their own borders. The ECPG gained the impression that the Japanese seemed to enjoy their quasi-white status inside South Africa.

Violence

In certain quarters the ECPG heard the argument that sanctions would lead to greater violence. However, the ECPG suspected that within this perspective there lurked a view that a black-dominated regime in South Africa would be even more violent against whites. Likewise, it detected a racial dimension to the non-violence argument. Where white pro-Westerners are in power, the West demands that opposition to them be non-violent. But, if those in power do not belong to the white Western establishment, then arms and money can be given for the violent overthrow of such governments without much moral compunction, witness the cases of Nicaragua, Afghanistan, Angola, and Mozambique.

The ECPG unequivocally condemned the escalating violence in Southern Africa as a whole but asked who was responsible for this violence in South Africa, Namibia, and the Frontline States? It argued that blame had to be put on the shoulders of the regime in South Africa. Why then do these Western Christian advocates of non-violence, who condemn the 'violence' of the ANC, not, with the same vehemence, condemn the institutionalized violence of the white apartheid regime? Why is it that Western governments are not so perturbed when a white racist regime criminalizes peaceful non-violent protest, while the regime's warlike, violent, inhuman injustice gets legal protection? Why is that conscience not outraged by states of emergency, forced removals and imprisonments, torture and illegal detention, by the sending of troops into black townships to terrorize its occupants and shoot unarmed men, women and children?

The ECPG's position was consistently this: there is endemic and oppressive white violence in South Africa. This has generated the counter-violence of the oppressed. If both are left unchecked, the result will be a cruel bloodbath. The only non-violent means left to the international community to put an end to violence and to avoid the bloodbath is effective multi-lateral, comprehensive sanctions which would non-violently force the undemocratic minority government to the negotiating table.

Communism

The baseless fear of black violence is exacerbated by another bogey — the spectre of communism. It is all too easy to paint all liberation movements as marxist and communist. The un-informed can be easily scared by propaganda to the effect that, if these liberation movements come to power, they will immediately nationalize all land and industry. The liberation movements are often accused of being pro-communist and of receiving financial assistance from the Soviet Union. Seldom is there an effort to ascertain the proportion of such assistance from the Soviet Union compared to other countries. The question is not asked whether the liberation movements have been offered and refused assistance from the West.

The upholders of apartheid play upon the susceptibilities of Western Christians by arguing that it is important to keep South Africa as a strategic geo-political entity within the Western camp and not to let it go over to the 'enemy'. However, with the prevailing mood of detente between Western governments and the USSR under President Gorbachev this shibboleth should be laid to rest.

The Free Enterprise Interest

Another fear which the ECPG detected was that a free democratic South Africa would be lost to the Western market system. Many, however, in the international business community are now detecting the fallacy in the argument. The fact is that to support the perpetuation of apartheid is to alienate the black majority and risk losing that market in the democratic South Africa of the future. If the international business community, on the other hand, supported sanctions to dismantle apartheid, an independent democratic South Africa would likely remain open to the 'free enterprise' world. The greatest guarantee for future business security will be a stable, non-racial, democratic South Africa.

The ECPG also heard the same argument from nearly all the governments visited, namely that theirs was a free enterprise economy and they could not make banks and corporations act as they wished. While this may be legally true, strong leadership and co-ordinated action by Western governments and business communities could quickly put an end to apartheid. It is essentially a question of priorities.

Apartheid as a Crime Against Humanity

Not all governments of the countries visited had ratified the International Convention on the Suppression and Punishment of the Crime of Apartheid adopted by the United Nations in 1973. Nonetheless consensus in UN circles and world public opinion on that question has been developing. The business community, however, has been slow to recognize the moral aspects of dealing with a criminal regime. Some state leaders were content to leave market forces to take care of the problem of apartheid.

Apartheid is a crime, and the apartheid regime is a criminal regime. It kills people — men, women and children created in the image of God — in South Africa as well as in neighbouring countries. It inflicts hunger, malnutrition and undernourishment which stunts the growth of hundreds of thousands of children. It separates families. It tortures and detains people without trial. Many die in prison under inhuman conditions. It humiliates human beings and tramples upon their God-given dignity. Is it Judaeo-Christian morality to leave the ending of these excesses to 'market forces'? Why can the West not use its moral force and persuasive power to remove this blot and bring relief and liberation to millions, whether Christians, Moslems or unbelievers?

Apartheid as a crime is a challenge to Western civilization and European Christianity. Most of those who do business with South Africa claim to be upholders of Western civilization. At the political and ideological level, in as much as Western nations claim to believe in the principles of democracy — that all people are created equal in the sight of God and have rights which inherently derive from that fact which civilized government must protect — then they need to conduct their foreign relations and trading interests in ways which are consistent with that principle. They ascribe to the Universal Declaration of Human Rights that guarantees freedom to all regardless of colour, race, religion or creed. The Declaration — a fundamental of Western civilization — guarantees freedom of speech and assembly.

South Africa claims to ascribe to the principles of Western Christian civilization, yet violates its fundamental principles. With impunity, it flouts all those principles using brutal repression. Yet Western and Japanese corporations trade with South Africa and accrue profit off the exploitation of the black majority. Is profit so important that the moral factor can be ignored? Most Western business leaders claim to be Christians whose religion imposes an obligation on them not to 'sup with the devil'. Apartheid is a sin, and Christians neither reform nor compromise with sin.

14. Conclusions

Even as the ECPG undertook its mission, the situation in South Africa deteriorated still further. As the mission ended, the state of emergency was almost 1,000 days old and thousands of people were still in detention, neither charged nor tried. Hundreds were on hunger strike demanding to be tried or released; those that were released were placed under severe restrictions requiring them to report to the police twice a day, remain in their houses at night, and not address meetings or be interviewed.

The hour in South Africa is late; it is one minute to midnight and fraught with danger. The ECPG fully recognized the urgency of the situation. It undertook its mission in an attempt to alert South Africa's major trading partners to the catastrophe that will overtake that country unless comprehensive mandatory sanctions are imposed and monitoring mechanisms adopted to ensure that sanctions are not broken.

In South Africa the majority has unequivocally rejected the government's so-called reform programme, which they regard as a cosmetic attempt to give apartheid a human face. Apartheid, they argue, is an unbridled repressive tyranny which cannot be reformed; it must be dismantled.

A dangerous collision looms ahead. Such a collision will be a catastrophic tragedy for South Africa and the Frontline States. It will also affect race relations around the world. The tragedy can be avoided by the imposition of comprehensive mandatory sanctions, the only effective means now available to the international community.

Sanctions work. That is why the South African government fears them. Mr Barend du Plessis, the South African Minister of Finance, told Parliament on 15 March 1989 that international sanctions were hurting the country's economy:

> Every South African will have to make a sacrifice in the battle against an economic onslaught which is being organized against the country internationally. . . . To abolish the financial rand now would simply mean that the country would lose much by way of foreign reserves and moreover would have to accept a sharp depreciation of the commercial rand (*International Herald Tribune*, 16.3.89).

The ECPG is deeply concerned about the explosive situation in South Africa. For the black majority there can be no more compromise with apartheid nor a return to the past where a situation of live and let live was sometimes adopted after major explosions like Sharpeville in 1960. Since 1984 the black majority has displayed enormous determination to end the system that has brutalized and humiliated them for so long. Those who claim to have some leverage with the South African government are not aiding the situation by refusing to impose stronger sanctions.

The ECPG was concerned at the laxity of some governments in their dealings with, and their prognosis for the future of, South Africa. The lack of urgency, the sit-back attitude, of many governments dismayed the ECPG. The failure to realize the urgency of the situation distressed the ECPG which sensed that the attitude of these governments contributed to the confidence of the apartheid regime that the major industrialized countries would not adopt decisive economic measures against it. In many countries, the ECPG noted the double standard of condemning apartheid as immoral and yet continuing business-as-usual to sustain the system. The economy of South Africa and the apartheid system survive largely on the trade between it and the major industrialized countries.

The Commonwealth Eminent Persons Group (EPG) reported that it 'was forcibly struck by the overwhelming desire in the country for a non-violent negotiated settlement. The onus rested on the government, as the wielders of police and military power, to introduce a climate in which negotiations involving all sections of political opinion could take place on the basis of equality without let, hindrance or fear of harassment' (p. 99). The EPG argued that comprehensive mandatory sanctions would help produce a climate that would facilitate negotiations to resolve the South African problem. Of such sanctions, the Commonwealth Eminent Persons Group reported: 'It is not whether such measures will compel change; it is already the case that their absence and Pretoria's belief that they need not be feared, defers change' (p. 140). The Report concluded by stating that, unless stronger sanctions were imposed, the world faced the prospect of the 'worst bloodbath since the Second World War' (p. 141). Ultimately, the EPG felt that the failure to impose stronger economic measures against South Africa worked against the deeply felt desire by the majority in that country for a non-violent negotiated settlement.

We in the ECPG appeal to all Churches to raise loudly their prophetic voice against apartheid within the national and international contexts. The Churches must pool their resources and express their solidarity with the oppressed people of South Africa. In setting up the ECPG, the WCC has once again demonstrated its leading international role in the struggle against apartheid. Churches in their local and national situations must assume a similar leading role, not just denouncing apartheid but taking and advocating concrete steps to end it. The ECPG is convinced that determined actions by the Churches can help bring out, sooner and not later, a non-racial, unitary, democratic South Africa where neither race, colour nor creed with determine the lives and destiny of the people of that beautiful country.

15. Recommendations of the Eminent Church Persons Group

We urge the General Secretary of the WCC to arrange for further high-level visits and continuing contacts with governments, inter-governmental agencies, member churches and affiliated councils of churches, as well as with the business community, thereby placing before them the concerns of the ECPG, and to give special attention to:

(1) The responsibility of member churches to adopt anti-apartheid action plans in collaboration with other activist groups in order to create maximum pressure on their respective governments to:

a) adopt comprehensive mandatory sanctions against South Africa;

b) ratify the International Convention on the Suppression and Punishment of the Crime of Apartheid;

c) fully implement those sanctions which currently exist.

(2) An early meeting with the President of the European Community to request the adoption by the EEC of decisive economic measures — with specific focus on oil, coal and ending South African Airways' landing rights as a means to pressure the South African Government to end repressive apartheid laws. These measures should be placed on the agenda of the Council of Ministers.

(3) A meeting with the Prime Minister of Canada to reinforce

the important role Canada plays in Commonwealth and Security Council discussions; and to urge it to maintain its strong support for sanctions, perceived in some quarters now to be weakening.

(4) Meetings with the banking community with a specific focus on the committee of 14 banks responsible for renegotiating the loans to South Africa so as to convey the convictions of the Eminent Church Persons Group regarding bank loans and to use the rescheduling of loans due in 1990 as a means of pressure on the South African government.

(5) Put pressure on the international media to take creative steps to overcome the present absence of media coverage on South Africa in a period of increased repression. Likewise, local and national church leaders should meet with editorial boards of the major newspapers as part of the church media network undertaking an active commitment to redress this imbalance.

(6) Undertaking a careful monitoring of the implementation of UN Resolution 435 to ensure free elections and a truly free Namibia as well as pressurizing UNTAG to maintain a presence at sufficient levels to deter South African disruption of the independence process.

It is our fervent hope that a non-racial democratic society may be negotiated by peaceful means. These recommendations are intended to support this commitment.

Appendix

**The ECPG's Programme of Visits and Meetings,
13 January – 7 February 1989**

Geneva, Switzerland	13 – 15 January
Bern, Switzerland	15 – 17 January
Paris, France *and*	
Brussels, Belgium	17 – 19 January
London, UK	19 – 24 January
Bonn, FRG	24 – 26 January
Tokyo, Japan	27 – 30 January
Washington, DC, USA	30 January – 2 February
New York, USA	2 – 3 February
Geneva	5 – 7 February

January 16

Bern, Switzerland

— News Conference
— Ambassador Alfred Ruegg of the Ministry of Foreign
 Affairs
— Swiss Protestant Church Federation

January 17

Paris, France

Rev. Dr Canaan Banana, Metropolitan Dr Paulos Mar

Gregorios and Dr James Mutambirwa met with:

— DEFAP (French Department of Apostolic Action)
— CIMADE (Comité Inter-Mouvement d'Aide aux Evacués)

January 18

— Mouvement anti-apartheid
— M François Scheer, General Secretary of the Quai d'Orsay, Ministry of Foreign Affairs
— M Jean-Christophe Mitterrand, specialist on African Affairs in the President's Office — Champs-Elysées
— M Jacques Desponts, International Affairs, Ministry of Trade and Finance
— M Christian Lechervy, CCFD (Catholic Committee Against Hunger and for Development)
— Representatives of DEFAP and CEEVA (Evangelical Community of Apostolic Action)

January 19

— M Laurent Fabius, President of the National Assembly

Later that day Metropolitan Gregorios and James Mutambirwa met:

— M Philippe Petit, Technical Advisor to the Prime Minister on Foreign Affairs

January 18

Brussels, Belgium

Ms Elaine Hesse Greif, Dr Lysaneas Maciel, Rev. Frank Chikane and Rev. Bob Scott met with:

— The Ecumenical Group
— Representatives of NGOs
— Press Conference

January 19

— M Reyn, Chef de Cabinet, Ministry of Foreign Affairs

131

January 20

London, UK

— Archbishop of Canterbury, the Most Rev. Dr Robert Runcie at Lambeth Palace
— Representatives of the ANC
— Chief Emeka Anyaoku, Commonwealth Secretariat

January 22

— Paul Boateng MP, Vice-Moderator, Commission on the Programme to Combat Racism

January 23

— Sir Geoffrey Howe, Foreign and Commonwealth Secretary
— Mr Gerald Kaufman MP and Labour Shadow Foreign Secretary
— Anti-Apartheid Movement
— British Council of Churches
— Press Conference
— Representatives of PAC

January 24

Bonn, West Germany

— 150 members of Parishes and Action Groups at the Evangelical Mulheim Academy, including:

  — Plädoyer für eine ökumenische Zukunft
  — Anti-Apartheids-Bewegung
  — Arbeitskreis 'Kein Geld für Apartheid'
  — Evangelische Frauenarbeit im Deutschland
  — Mainzer Arbeitskreis 'Südliches Afrika'
  — Arbeitskreis 'Südafrika im Ruhrgebiet'
  — Solidarische Kirche im Rheinland
  — Südafrika-Kreis im Kirchenkreis Oberhausen
  — Gewerkschaft Handel, Banken und Versicherungen
  — Südafrikaner im Exil

January 25

Dusseldorf

— Ernest Breit, Chairman of the German Trade Union Congress (DGB)
— Members of the Executive, Evangelical Church in the Rhineland

Bonn

— Hans Dietrich Genscher, Foreign Minister
— President Richard von Weizsäcker
— Council of EKD and EMW

January 26

— Chancellor Helmut Kohl
— ANC representative, Tony Seedat
— SWAPO representative, Nghidimondjila Shoombe
— Dr Hans Stercken, Chairman of Committee for Foreign Affairs of the Bundestag
— Social Democratic MPs: Mrs Totemeyer and Mr Verhengen

January 27

Tokyo, Japan

— National Council of Churches
— Japan Anti-Apartheid Committee

January 28

— News Conference
— Reception with church leaders, officials of Christian Council of Japan, Japan Anti-Apartheid Committee, representatives of the African Diplomatic Corps, the ANC representative in Japan
— 45 church leaders

January 29

Rally addressed by Rev. Canaan Banana and Rev. Frank Chikane

January 30

— Mr Takamori Makino, Vice-Minister of Foreign Affairs
— Mr Takasho Onda, Director General of the Middle East and African Affairs Office, Ministry of Foreign Affairs
— Ms Takado Doi, Chairwoman of Japan's Socialist Party
— News Conference

January 31

Washington, USA

— James Baker III, US Secretary of State
— Damu Smith, Executive Director, Washington Office on Africa

February 1

— Randall Robinson, Executive Director, Trans Africa
— Senate and House Foreign Policy Staff, Dirksen Senate Office Building
— Mr Youssefou, OAU Ambassador to the United Nations
— Gay Macdougall, Director, Lawyers Committee for Civil Rights Under Law, Southern Africa Project
— Hearings/Reception sponsored by National Council of Churches, Washington Church Office Heads, Washington Office on Africa, IMPACT and United Church of Christ

February 2

— Representative Ronald Dellums, Chair, Congressional Black Caucus, Rayburn Office Building with Rep. Dante Fascell, Chair House Foreign Affairs Committee and Rep. Mervyn Dymally, former Chair, Congressional Black Caucus
— Press Conference
— Canadian church leaders
— Senator Nancy Kassebaum (Republican, Kansas) and Senator Richard Lugar (Republican, Indiana) Russel Senate Office Building
— Senator Paul Simon (Democrat, Illinois), Senator Claiborne Pell, Chair Senate Foreign Relations Committee and Alan

Cranston, sponsor, Comprehensive Anti-Apartheid Act of 1988 — Dirksen Senate Office Building
— Senator Edward Kennedy, Russel Senate Office Building
— Sarah Sewell, Southern Africa specialist for Senator George J. Mitchell (Democrat), Senate Majority leader — Capitol Building

February 3

New York

— News briefing with United Nations Correspondents Association
— New York Times
— UN Secretary-General Perez de Cuellar
— UN Special Committee Against Apartheid
— News Conference, Interchurch Center
— Dialogue with church, labour and anti-apartheid groups:
   — Patrice Lumumba Coalition
   — United Church Board for World Ministries, Co-Chairperson United Church of Christ Divestment, Implementation Committee
   — Secretary for Africa, United Church Board for World Ministries
   — American Baptists Church, USA, Director, Social & Ethical Responsibility in Investments
   — United Methodist Church, Director of the United Nations Office
   — YMCA
   — The Black Council of the Reformed Church in America
   — Presbyterian Church (USA)
   — Episcopal Church
   — Executive Director of Interfaith Center on Corporate Responsibility (ICCR), Director South Africa Program ICCR
   — National Catholic Office